Principles f
the Proper

INTERPRETING
THE HOLY SCRIPTURES

by Herbert T. Mayer
Concordia Theological Seminary
St. Louis, Missouri

Concordia
Leadership
Training Series

Concordia Publishing House
St. Louis, Missouri

Concordia Publishing House, St. Louis, Missouri
Concordia Publishing House Ltd., London, E. C. 1
Copyright 1967 by Concordia Publishing House
Fourth Printing 1969
MANUFACTURED IN THE UNITED STATES OF AMERICA

Principles for a proper study and use of the Bible have always been important to the life of the church and its message to the world, as also this study text indicates. The reformation of the church in any age cannot take place without a serious reexamination of the foundations and norm of the church in its sacred Scriptures, the Word of God. Such study requires honest and prayerful observance of sound principles of *hermeneutics,* meaning the science of interpretation and of *Biblical* translation and explanation in particular.

Today these principles and the truths of the Bible that they serve to uncover or establish are being sharpened and called into use by a variety of theological questions. In regard to texts of the Bible and traditional dogma that may or may not be based on a Word of Scripture, the truth of the matter can be established only by the study of the Biblical Word. And this study, to be valid, must proceed according to the nature of the Scriptures and the practical methods that lead to their original God-intended meanings.

Present-day interest in principles of Biblical interpretation has been "provoked" largely by controversies of one kind or another. *Far more important is the need of the application of sound principles in the personal use and teaching of the Bible*. All of us know how others (if we have failed to see the beam in our own eyes) have misused Biblical texts or have allowed false or unwarranted teachings to take on the authority of God's Word.

Especially the teachers of the church (also the lay teachers of children, youth, or adults) must be able to rightly discern and interpret the Word of Truth and to guard against a careless, misperceived, prejudiced, inaccurate, false, or sentimental teaching of the Bible. A concern for a true interpretation and use of the Bible is a concern for the truth of God. Without this concern one cannot truly serve God, no matter how much one might quote or refer to the Bible.

For this reason the Leadership Training Committee of our Board of Parish Education is grateful to God that it is able to add this course by Prof. Herbert T. Mayer of Concordia Seminary, St. Louis, to its Leadership Training Program for church school teachers and others. This book is probably the first attempt at providing a brief and nontechnical course on this very important subject. An Instructors Guide is available as an aid for the formal teaching of this text in an accredited leadership training course in the parish or in interparish institutes.

To be able to recommend the private or group study of this book increases my hope for the coming of our Lord's kingdom through His church.

ALLAN HART JAHSMANN
General Secretary of Sunday Schools
The Lutheran Church — Missouri Synod

CONTENTS

Introduction

This book deals with methods of studying and interpreting the Bible. Because Christians place great emphasis upon Biblical teachings, they need to be confident that they understand the Bible properly. The purpose of this course is to help Bible teachers and students become better Bible interpreters.

Some Definitions

The science of Biblical interpretation is called "hermeneutics" (her-meh-neu'-tiks), from the Greek word *hermeneuein* (her-meh-neu'-ein), which means "to translate, explain, or interpret." The use of hermeneutical principles to explain the meaning of Scripture is called "exegesis" (ek-seh-je'-sis). This comes from two Greek words and means "to guide out" or "to lead out"; that is, to bring out the meaning which the Spirit of God put into the Biblical text.

Courses in hermeneutics at seminaries are often called "Principles of Biblical Interpretation." This course will emphasize principles (hermeneutics) rather than the interpretation of specific passages (exegesis). But it will of course be necessary to show how principles work, so there will be many examples of exegesis scattered throughout the course.

A Word of Caution

An important word of caution is needed at the outset. The student ought not to expect that the completion of this course will end all his questions about the meaning of every verse or pericope (a selection of several verses). The guidelines of interpretation that will be studied by no means guarantee a quick and sure-fire explanation of any and every text. Exegetes who use the same basic principles may still disagree about the meaning of some passages. Chapter 2 will provide examples of how serious and sound exegetes have differed in the past.

But the mastery of sound principles will prove very helpful to the Christian who will pray sincerely for God's guidance and will try hard to understand what God is saying to him in a given passage. Hermeneutics is an art rather than an exact science such as physics or chemistry. Like an artist, the good exegete must develop a sensitivity and feel for his subject. This sensitivity comes as the Bible student saturates himself with Scripture and becomes personally familiar with it.

Above all, good exegesis depends on the guidance and illumination of the Holy Spirit. Before His death Jesus promised to give the Spirit of God to His disciples so that He (the Spirit) could teach them all things and bring to their remembrance all that Jesus had said to them (John 14:26). Because the Bible is a book of "Spirit-ual" truths, it can be understood rightly only by those who are taught by the Spirit (1 Cor. 2:9-16). This is a cardinal principle of Biblical interpretation.

In addition, a good hermeneutical system is important because it enables the reader to determine more accurately and more fully what God is saying to him in a given portion of the Bible. Because God has graciously chosen to communicate with His children in written form, they are naturally interested in understanding correctly His Word to them.

In view of man's persistent rebellion against his Creator, it is a marvel of grace that God speaks to human beings in any form. But He has spoken and continues to speak to His creatures in various ways.

Before one begins to study the Bible, the written Word of God to man, it is well to have a clear understanding of the various ways in which God speaks. This knowledge, in turn, may help the reader to understand and interpret the Bible. History and experience show that an adequate understanding of the nature of the Word of God and of the Bible is essential to sound Bible study.

The Meaning of "Word of God"

The statement "The Bible is the Word of God" is loaded with rich theological freight. To understand all that this phrase can mean, it is necessary to understand the term "Word of God." To many this term seems to require no study or explanation. "The Word is the Word is the Word," they may be tempted to say.

But a study of the term "word" in the Bible will quickly show that it has several different basic meanings. Thus, "Word of God" (either *davar* in the Old Testament or *logos* in the New Testament) frequently has the meaning of force or activity. It can therefore mean the power by which God carries out His purposes. In the Old Testament, "Word of God" clearly means power or purpose in those passages where it is spoken of as the agent by which God created the world and still preserves it. (See Genesis 1; Ps. 33:4-6; Ps. 147:15-19.)

Deut. 8:3 is a very important passage for understanding the meaning of "Word of God." It reads: "Man does not live by bread alone, but man lives by everything (*davar*) that proceeds out of the mouth of the Lord." Our

Lord quoted these words when he was tempted by the devil (Matt. 4:4). Here "Word of God" means the will and power of God by which He can sustain His children even without food. In Is. 55:7-13 God describes His Word as a power that goes forth from Himself to accomplish what He pleases.

This understanding of the Word of God as the *power* of God is inherent in many New Testament passages also. The statement in Acts 6:7 is striking: "And the Word of God increased; and the number of the disciples multiplied greatly in Jerusalem." (See also Acts 12:24; 19:20; 20:32; Luke 1:37; John 5:24; 6:63; 1 Tim. 4:5; Heb. 11:3; 1 Peter 1:23-25.) In a comment on the 1 Peter passage, Luther said: "The Word is a divine power; yes, it is God Himself."

In the well-known John 1:1-14 passage, "Word" clearly means Jesus Christ — God incarnate. "In the beginning was the Word . . . and the Word was God. . . . And the Word became flesh and dwelt among us." (See also Rev. 19:13; John 4:31-36.) Heb. 1:1-2 describes Jesus as God's greatest and final Word: "In many and various ways God spoke of old to our fathers by the prophets; but in these last days He has spoken to us by a Son, whom He appointed the heir of all things, through whom also He created the world." Allan Hart Jahsmann has correctly concluded that "In the fullest sense of the term, Jesus Christ is the Word — the revelation of God." (*How You Too Can Teach* [St. Louis: Concordia, 1963] p. 25)

In other places in the Bible, "word" means that which God's Spirit caused to be spoken or written down (2 Chron. 34:21; Jer. 25:13; 30:1-3). God instructed Jeremiah to take a scroll and to write on it all the words which He had spoken against Israel, Judah, and all the nations of that time (Jer. 36:2). Moses encouraged the people of Israel to keep the words which God had given to him in written form (Deut. 11:8; see also Deut. 4:2; 17:19). In general, the term "Word of God" refers to the entire content of the Scriptures, both

Law and Gospel. This Word of proclamation (both Law and Gospel) is sometimes called Law in the broad sense and sometimes Gospel.

In the New Testament Peter described the entire Old Testament as "the prophetic word made more sure" (2 Peter 1:19). In other New Testament passages, "word" is frequently a shorthand symbol for the life, death, resurrection, and saving work of Jesus Christ (Acts 8:4-5), that which today is commonly called the Gospel, the message (good news) of God's salvation in Jesus Christ (Eph. 1: 13; Phil. 2:16; Col. 1:3-7). It is important to note that in these passages the Word is described as possessing the power to restore peace between man and God (2 Cor. 5: 16-21), to cleanse the church (Eph. 5:25-27), and so forth, so it is, again, the "power" of God—for life and salvation. (Acts 20:32; Rom. 1:16)

The Word of God as Revelation

An understanding of the meaning of revelation also is important to a full understanding of the term "Word of God." In Biblical usage revelation means the making known of something which would have remained hidden and unknown if God had not proclaimed it in some manner. Revelation thus defined includes such things as dreams and visions given to the prophets, the birth and life of Jesus, and a long list of mighty acts which God performed in the history of Israel and their surrounding nations. Thus understood, one can view the Bible as *containing* reports about God's revelation while at the same time *being* revelation.

The Bible devotes considerable space especially to five events by which God helped His people and taught them many truths about Himself. These "mighty acts of God," as they are called, were (1) the creation and preservation of the world; (2) the exodus of the Israelites from Egypt and the giving of the law at Mount Sinai; (3) the exile of

Israel and their return from Babylonia; (4) the incarnation, life, death, and resurrection of Jesus Christ; and (5) the outpouring of the Holy Spirit and the creation of the new Israel, the Christian church, on Pentecost and in the years that followed.

When God acted, or as the Bible expresses it, when He spoke or sent forth His Word to produce action, He often caused men and women to explain the meaning of His action to the people. Furthermore, God also inspired prophets and apostles to *write* the account of His great deeds and the explanation of their meaning. Much of the Bible, then, is the inspired record of and witness to God's revelation of Himself through His mighty acts. Many chapters in the Bible report how His people later meditated upon these acts and found guidance, faith, and strength for their own day. (Ps. 135 and 136 are two examples.)

God's Spirit also *preserved* the accounts and the explanations of those mighty acts so that His people in later ages could have a clear and dramatic presentation of God's nature and will and His ways of dealing with people. This in turn enabled later generations to hear and learn of God's acts for His people in the past so that through this recorded Word God's Spirit could call forth responses of faith and obedience from His people in every age. God's past revelations in His proclamations and dealings with people are converted by the Spirit into present revelations.

The Word of God and the Bible

Our brief study of the term "Word of God" has called attention to four important meanings which it has in the Bible. It can mean the power or force of God; it can mean Jesus Christ; it can mean the story of the redemptive work of Jesus Christ; and it can mean the Bible itself. In all these meanings God seeks out man to communicate to him forgiveness of sins, blessings, and salvation—that is, His Word of life.

The main purpose for which God gave the Bible can, then, be stated simply. Through it God speaks to people, telling them about Himself and about what He has done for them in Jesus Christ so that the Holy Spirit can create saving faith in the reader, hearer, and learner: "From childhood you have been acquainted with the sacred writings which are able to instruct you for salvation through faith in Christ Jesus" (2 Tim. 3:15). The words of the Bible have this great and marvelous power because the Spirit of God works through them.

It is of course also true that men can say "No" to God's call to them, but because the Bible is God's Word, God's action, they cannot evade a decision. So the Bible student, dealing with the Word of God, must keep in mind that he is working with something which is alive and powerful. "The Word of God is something alive and active: it cuts like any double-edged sword but more finely; it can slip through the place where the soul is divided from the spirit, or joints from the marrow; it can judge the secret emotions and thoughts" (Heb. 4:12, Jerusalem Bible). This indicates that genuine Bible study is literally a "life and death" matter. Furthermore, the believing Christian regards the Bible with deep respect and submits himself to the teachings of the Bible. Refusing to become a judge of the Bible, he is happy to confess that the Bible is authoritative for his life and thought.

At the same time the Bible student must remember that he is studying a book which is essentially sacred history, the history of the mighty acts of judgment and deliverance performed by God for His people in the days of old. This history becomes the Bible student's personal history through faith, for then he finds himself personally involved in God's dealings with His people, especially through Jesus Christ.

For 16 centuries after the time of Christ, Christians rarely raised questions about the inspiration of the Bible. St. Paul taught that "all Scripture [for him this meant the Old Testament since there was no New Testament in his time] is inspired by God." Because it is inspired, God-breathed, Paul went on to say that it is "profitable for teaching, for reproof, for correction, and for training in righteousness, that the man of God may be complete, equipped for every good work" (2 Tim. 3:16-17). Note that the apostle bases a very practical observation about the value and power of Scripture on the fact of inspiration.

The other writers of the New Testament and of the early church say very little about inspiration. They were much more concerned about the trustworthiness and the authority of these sacred writings. Instead of maintaining that a book was inspired, they emphasized other characteristics. In general they insisted that only books written by apostles or by a disciple of an apostle were entitled to a special position of honor among the Christian writings. Or they gave special prominence to those books which had been used from the earliest days by large numbers of Christian congregations. Many also insisted that a book must speak clearly and directly of Jesus Christ if it were to be regarded as a special gift of God's Spirit to the church. By A. D. 200 most of the books which we today call canonical and inspired had achieved a place of unique importance in the life of the Christian church.

Until the time of the Enlightenment in European thought (A. D. 1700), serious questions about the inspiration and authority of the 66 canonical books were seldom raised. Christians affirmed the inspiration of the Bible without fear of contradiction. During the past 4 centuries, however, the inspiration of the Bible has become a center of discussion and controversy in the church.

The doctrine of inspiration was denied, for example, by some men of the Enlightenment who argued that God would not inspire a book whose teachings would then limit Him. Others said that the Bible was so quaint and curious, so old-fashioned, that it could not have been inspired by an ever-living God. Still others pointed to apparent contradictions and errors in the Bible and on this basis denied its inspiration. They pointed out, for example, that the books of Samuel (2 Sam. 10:18) and Chronicles (1 Chron. 19:18) give different figures for soldiers killed in the same battle; or that the Gospel writers report different words on Pilate's bulletin on the cross; and so forth. Some of these scholars taught that it was the task of the Bible interpreter to find the genuine words of God among the error-filled words of the human authors.

To answer these attacks and to settle some questions in their own minds, Christian theologians in many denominations have worked out definitions of inspiration which stoutly echo St. Paul's statement that all Scripture [including also the New Testament] is inspired by God. This same truth is stated in 2 Peter 1:20-21: "No prophecy ever came by the impulse of man, but men moved by the Holy Spirit spoke from God."

The prophets of the Old Testament insist again and again that they have had a word or a dream or a vision from God that they are to deliver to the people (Jer. 1:2; Hos. 1:1; Joel 1:1; etc.). The prophet of the New Testament, St. John of the Apocalypse (Revelation), concludes his book with a very solemn claim that his writing is God's Word. "I warn every one who hears the words of the prophecy of this book: if any one adds to them, God will add to him the plagues described in this book, and if anyone takes away from the words of the book of this prophecy, God will take away his share in the tree of life and in the holy city, which are described in this book." (Rev. 22:18-19)

But the Bible tells us practically nothing of how the holy writers received their words from God. Some prophets say that they were caught up bodily when they received revelatory visions (Ezek. 37), but ordinarily the prophets simply state that the revelatory Word of the Lord came to them and make no attempt to describe the spiritual or psychological process. (Ezek. 38:1; Jer. 3:6)

Most of the passages mentioned in the preceding paragraph describe revelation, that process by which God communicates divine truth and understanding to man. They do not describe inspiration, that process by which the Holy Spirit led a writer to write down what God had revealed to him. The Holy Spirit often inspired an author to write only after a previous revelation had taken place (Eph. 3:1-7). While revelation and inspiration are closely related, they are not the same.

Views of Inspiration

Because the Bible says so little about God's method of inspiration, the Bible student must content himself with the fact of inspiration and refuse to engage in long debates about the manner.

Over the centuries Christian theologians have advanced various theories of how inspiration might have worked. Many believed that the inspired writer was nothing more than a pen in the hands of the Holy Spirit. Some thinkers in the early church compared the Biblical writers to a flute into which the Holy Spirit blew to produce the music He wanted to create. This opinion, called the "dictation" theory, reflected a very pious and reverent view of the authority and reliability of the Bible, but it went beyond the Biblical information and failed to explain the unique varieties of ideas, styles, thought patterns, and emphases which are found in the Bible.

Even a quick reading of the New Testament will reveal very noticeable differences in the four Gospels or in the epistles. Matthew differs noticeably from Luke or Mark in style of writing, range of thought, choice of stories, and so forth. James's epistle is different from the writing of Peter. These obvious differences demand a definition of Biblical inspiration which gives an influential role also to the human authors.

Some theologians have solved this difficult problem of the relationship of the inspiring Spirit to the human writers by calling the Holy Spirit the *primary* Author and the inspired writer the *secondary* author. These terms affirm the absolutely essential role of the Spirit of God while also acknowledging the very obvious effects which the writer's personality and thought had upon his product. The human writers reflected upon and "searched and inquired about" the Spirit's message even as they wrote it under his direction (1 Peter 1:10-12). The problem of apparent contradictions and errors is discussed in Chapters 4 to 6.

Many Christians find this theory of inspiration hard to understand and accept. It seems to them that one must either accept some form of the mechanical dictation theory or else, to be logical, one must say that human beings wrote the Biblical books by themselves. Others maintain that if the second view is correct, then the Bible loses all of its divine character and its divine authority and trustworthiness.

How the divine and the human are joined in the Bible is really no easier to explain than the related question of how the divine and human were joined in the God-man Jesus Christ. But the fact is that this union occurred in both cases. The Bible makes its divine origin and nature plain to every believing student. But it also has a distinctly human origin and nature. An understanding of this human aspect of the Scriptures also is absolutely necessary, as we shall see.

Because the Bible says practically nothing about the "how" of inspiration, it may be best to think of inspiration as St. Paul thought of it. He connected inspiration with a statement about the Bible's purpose, namely that the sacred writings were able to instruct him for salvation which is in Christ Jesus (2 Tim. 3:14-17). The inspiration of the Scriptures was God's way of giving us His Word in written form to accomplish the great purpose Paul mentions. The inspired Word serves God's Spirit as the means of creating faith in Jesus Christ and serves the believing Christian as his light for faith and life. And God's Word in written form, as in every other form, is truthful, inerrant and completely dependable.

How the Bible Came to Us

The original Biblical books and letters which the inspired authors wrote or dictated personally (autographs) have disappeared. The earliest copies thus far discovered date from 200 B. C. to A. D. 250. But today there are literally thousands of early hand-written copies of larger or smaller portions of the Bible available to Biblical scholars. While it is true that no two of these copies are completely the same, it is also true that general agreement among them is remarkably high. A study of the Revised Standard Version text and footnotes will introduce the reader to some of the more important differences in manuscript copies (variant readings).

Several points should be kept in mind as the student thinks about variant readings. A specific variation may occur in only a small number of manuscripts out of the dozens or hundreds of copies that have been found. Further, it is generally true that these variations do not affect any major teaching of Scripture or any narrative account. Then, too, textual criticism (the practice of determining the original reading) is quite exacting. Careful study of available manuscripts has led scholars to a rather common agreement as to how the original text read in most instances.

While scholars will continue to study and debate textual problems, especially when important manuscripts such as the Qumran scrolls are discovered, the English Bible student can use the King James or RSV text with confidence. The RSV text, which is based on many more manuscripts than the KJV, is usually more accurate. However, in using any translation, the Bible student must remember that every translation is some distance removed from the precise meaning of the original. The text of the New English Bible is also reliable as a whole, but no human translation is perfect and timeless. Therefore the study of various translations can be helpful.

One other observation should be made in this connection. God did not abandon the Scriptures after He had caused holy men to record His Word. We can be certain that the Spirit of God continues to watch over and preserve His Word, even as He promised to explain it to Christians. The Holy Spirit is present and active as men ask Him to guide them in the preparation of translations. While each translation has its own strengths and weaknesses, those which large segments of the Christian church have used and endorsed can be used with confidence by those Bible students who work only with their native language.

Summary

This chapter concerned itself primarily with the nature of the Word of God. The various basic meanings of the term "Word of God" were analyzed. It was noted that "Word of God" can mean the power or activity of God. Second, "Word of God," in the final analysis, is always Jesus Christ and therefore God Himself. Third, "Word of God" can refer to the written words of the Bible or the Bible as a book because they are the vehicle of the Word. Fourth, "Word of God" means the Gospel of Jesus Christ, the Word of God's truth, the message of salvation and the inspired truths or doctrines of life.

Through His Word God comes to man to reveal His judgment on sin but also His grace and love. He comes in His Word to create faith in Jesus Christ. Thus the Bible is a book with a unique power and purpose.

Revelation was explained as God's act in telling people something about Himself through His acts or His words or both. Inspiration was described as the mysterious process by which God's Spirit "moved" and directed the writers of the books of the Bible. Inspiration, rightly understood, does not, however, rule out the personality and mind of the human writer.

TO HELP YOU REVIEW

1. Give a definition of hermeneutics.

2. Give various important Biblical meanings of the expression "Word of God."

3. Comment on: "The Bible is the Word of God, but the Word of God is more than the Bible."

4. How can one distinguish between inspiration and revelation? Was the giving of the Law on Sinai revelation or inspiration? How about the birth of Jesus Christ?

5. How would you define "inspiration" when it refers to the Bible? Why have some denied inspiration?

6. Why is the dictation theory of inspiration not in accord with the Bible?

7. What basic purpose does the Word of God have in all its forms?

Christian theologians have given their finest talents to the interpretation of Scripture. In this work they have made use of a considerable variety of hermeneutical principles. A review of the history of Bible study provides invaluable information to the Bible student. Such history enables him to see how various methods of interpretation have developed and how some methods seem to lend themselves to abuse more readily than others.

Interpretation in the New Testament

The first Christian Bible students who left written examples of their work are the inspired authors of the New Testament books. They employed very specific hermeneutical principles in interpreting the Old Testament, although the various writers did not necessarily use the same methods.

In his interpretation of the Old Testament, Matthew used a hermeneutical principle which was quite revolutionary in his day. Under the inspiration of God's Spirit he maintained that the Old Testament, history and poetry as well as prophecy, pointed to Jesus of Nazareth as God's perfect Israelite and the Creator of the new Israel, the new people of God, the Christian church. The phrase,

"This was to fulfill" (or a similar expression), occurs 12 times in Matthew's Gospel. (For example, 2:15, 21:4, 27:9)

The Old Testament can be correctly understood, said Matthew, only by those who believe that everything God wants to do for mankind and all that He had been doing for the people of Israel was fulfilled in Jesus Christ. Matthew's boldness in using this principle is noteworthy in view of the fact that Jesus of Nazareth had been crucified for interpreting the Old Testament in the same manner.

The writer of the Letter to the Hebrews shared Matthew's conviction that the Old Testament could be correctly explained only in the light of Jesus Christ. But the Spirit led him to use a different hermeneutical principle to prove this point to his readers. His letter is a careful study of selected religious practices and experiences among the Israelites which, according to this writer, were imperfect and incomplete and were designed to point forward to the perfection of Jesus Christ.

Thus, in the Book of Hebrews the angels (chs. 1 and 2), high priests (chs. 3 – 5, 8), Melchizedek (chs. 6 and 7), the tabernacle (ch. 9), and Old Testament sacrifices (ch. 10) are used to indicate the greatness of Jesus. The principle of interpretation which the writer of the Book of Hebrews used was allegorical (typological) in nature. Both the Jews and the Greeks in Alexandria, Egypt, had employed this method to explain their religious writings, and this Christian author probably borrowed his method from them. Other examples of hermeneutical principles used by New Testament writers for explaining the Old Testament could be added.

The Pre-Reformation Era

The 3rd, 4th, and 5th centuries were a time of vigorous Bible study. The most brilliant and influential Bible student in the 3rd century was Origen, a professor of Bible at Alexandria, Egypt, and later at Caesarea in what today is called Palestine. He was a very capable textual critic, an expert on Palestinian geography, and the most gifted theologian of his day. While some of his theological opinions led to his condemnation for heresy after his death, his hermeneutical system influenced the church to the time of the Reformation.

Origen accepted the allegorical method which was used at Alexandria by Greek, Jewish, and Christian scholars alike. In essence this method assumes that a literary passage contains at least two truths or lessons. Origen favored the view that there were three meanings in each passage, and he quoted St. Paul's reference to the Thessalonians' "spirit and soul and body" (1 Thess. 5:23) to prove that his three-level method was Scriptural.

Origen believed that the Old Testament had to be interpreted allegorically in order to uncover its hidden Christian meaning in contrast to its obvious Jewish meaning. Allegorizing also helped Origen to explain many Old Testament passages which to this day appear to be difficult, crude, and even offensive to some readers.

One example of the allegorical method is his treatment of Joseph's many-colored coat. The first level of meaning, the "body" level (see 1 Thess. 5:23), was that Jacob made a special coat for his son. This was the only meaning that the majority of simple Christian Bible readers could see. But the second level, the "soul" level, was far more important. At this level the story contained a sharp moral warning against pride or favoritism. The third level, the mystical or "spiritual" level, however, was the most important. Here the coat stands for deep philosophical learning, and the 10 brothers are the evil men who want to drive all philosophy and learning out of the church. Only the best and wisest Christians, said Origen, could see the deepest or spiritual truth.

Bible scholars at Antioch in Syria rejected allegorical hermeneutics because it reduced Scripture to a "wax nose" which each interpreter could push and twist to make the Bible appear the way he wanted it to appear. But in spite of their protests, the method employed by Origen dominated the church's Bible interpreters for 1,200 years.

Why did this happen? What are the reasons for the continuing popularity of allegorical hermeneutics? (1) Its practitioners invariably display a profound respect for the Bible, and they are determined to understand the meaning of each phrase and word. (2) The method solves many difficult proplems of Biblical interpretation for those who ignore the plain meaning of the words. (3) The principle of various meanings in every passage seems to make the Bible a truly inexhaustible storehouse of spiritual truths. (4) It enables the preacher (or the Christian as such) to find texts which he can explain in a way that supports his point of view, even though the Bible becomes a "wax nose" and the interpreter is likely to become the determiner of the meaning of the Word of God.

In the period from A. D. 200 to 1500, a second development of hermeneutical significance was the appearance of creeds and confessions and the writings of revered church fathers. These are usually called "tradition." In some cases a confession of the church or a decree of a church council or the opinion of a church father was considered to be so fine and valuable that it became the official position of the western Christian church. It was no longer considered necessary to study the pertinent Bible passages underlying the statements and doctrines. The church had the final answer in its tradition.

Unfortunately, many traditional teachings and positions went beyond the teaching of the Bible and sometimes contradicted it. In an effort to break the stranglehold which tradition, both good and bad, had gotten upon the Bible, Peter Abelard (1079—1142) wrote a book called *Yes and No*. In this book he quoted councils and fathers against each other to show how dangerous it was to emphasize tradition and de-emphasize Bible study.

The Reformation and Bible Interpretation

Martin Luther (1483 — 1546)

Much of the power of the great reform movement associated with the name of Martin Luther flowed from his Bible study. His understanding of the nature of God and of God's communication to man in His Son Jesus Christ and in the Bible (see Ch. 1) led him to affirm many hermeneutical principles that had been forgotten in the church for centuries or were formulated for the first time by Luther. The new hermeneutical principles, in turn, made it possible for Luther to explain Scripture with such clarity and confidence that few, if any, Bible interpreters can be compared to him as an exegete.

Martin Luther held four firm beliefs concerning the nature of the Bible and its place in the life of the church. These formed the foundation upon which his hermeneutical system rested. First, like some who had preceded him, he believed that the Bible was the first and final source of authority in the church. While he respected tradition deeply and honored what councils and revered church fathers had taught in the past, he was not afraid to insist that even church councils could err and mislead people, while the Bible alone was inerrant and completely trustworthy.

Second, Luther taught that each pericope (passage or group of passages) of Scripture has only one meaning; and that the meaning God intended the church to get was always a single meaning. With this view he challenged almost all the other Bible students who had been trained in allegorical principles of interpretation. Furthermore Luther insisted against the allegorists that in general Scripture is clear. Its message can be understood by the simplest Christians. It is not a book which can be understood only by learned exegetes.

In the third place, said Luther, every Christian has the right of private judgment concerning the interpretation of

Bible passages. This principle has sometimes been misunderstood. Luther did not mean that every man could interpret the Bible in any way he pleased. This understanding could lead only to endless confusion among Christians. Rather, Luther meant that each Christian had the duty and the ability to test the teachings of the church to see if these teachings agreed with the Gospel of Jesus Christ (as did the Berean believers in Acts 17:10-12).

Fourth, Luther accepted and taught the Biblical interpretation endorsed by the church of his day unless that interpretation in some way obscured or confused the central doctrine of Scripture, the Gospel (see Apology of the Augsburg Confession, Articles VII and VIII 20.21; in the Tappert edition, see pp. 171f.). The hermeneutical principles which Luther developed on the basis of these beliefs will be discussed in Chapter 3.

John Calvin (1509—1564)

John Calvin, who is usually regarded as the direct or indirect founder of most Protestant churches, was perhaps a more thorough exegete than Luther, but he lacked the warmth and enthusiasm of his older contemporary. The hermeneutical systems of the two men are quite similar. Here the reader's attention will be called to only a few of Calvin's basic principles.

Like Luther, Calvin insisted that the Holy Spirit's guidance and illumination of the interpreter are absolutely essential. Calvin distinguished, perhaps more sharply than Luther, between the understanding which the first readers of a text may have had and the understanding that contemporary Bible readers may have. The *meaning* of a passage, said Calvin, is one and single, but the *understanding* held by readers in different ages or the *application* of the truth of the passage by Christians may change as their situations change.

Calvin insisted that the good Bible student must train himself to listen to the Biblical writer instead of making a passage support the ideas already held before a study of the text. Calvin is also remembered because he was never afraid to say that he did not understand what some Bible passages meant.

In the 16th and 17th Centuries

The pioneer work of Luther and Calvin was in part continued by their successors, such men as Philip Melanchthon (1497 – 1560). However the latter half of the 16th century is more noted for religious controversies than constructive Biblical studies. The Roman Catholic Church prepared herself for a counter-movement against Protestants by stating her beliefs, often in a belligerent fashion, in the Canons and Decrees of the Council of Trent (1545 – 1563). During this time the Protestants produced such confessions as the Augsburg Confession, the Formula of Concord, the Helvetic Confession, and others.

In this period Christians sometimes devoted more time and energy to refining and defining a system of Christian doctrine than they did to making sure they really understood what God wanted to say to them in His Word. Exegetes in this period sometimes also permitted their great learning and their desire for logical arrangement of religious truths to becloud what God was saying in a given passage. Furthermore, exegetes and theologians devoted countless hours to hair-splitting arguments in favor of their own system. Occasionally they seemed to think that they alone were correct and everyone else was a false teacher. Needless to say, much valuable Bible study went on in this period also.

Men like Philip Spener (1635 – 1705), August Hermann Francke (1663 – 1727), and Johann Albrecht Bengel (1687 – 1752) reacted against the narrowness and coldness of this immediate post-Reformation period. These men are usually called Pietists. They stressed that the Bible was spiritual food, to be read primarily for personal edification.

The Pietists placed great emphasis upon the study of the original Biblical languages and upon the application of Scripture to daily life. Unfortunately, pietist hermeneutics also led to abuses. Some Pietists paid little attention to the discipline of hermeneutics and the original meaning of the passage. They frequently permitted their emotions to decide what the Spirit of God was saying. In some circles Pietists almost ignored the Bible in favor of their personal feelings and emotions.

The Age of Enlightenment

The 18th and 19th centuries are sometimes called the Age of Enlightenment or the Age of Reason. It was a period of radical cultural change and mental upheaval. Nothing seemed to be too sacred to be analyzed, questioned, and even attacked. Leading thinkers like Thomas Hobbes (1588 – 1679) and Baruch Spinoza (1632 – 1677) taught that the human reason was capable of deciding what was true and false. Human reason, they said, could conquer any obstacle and solve any problem. Some of the rationalists felt that the church was against reason, so they set out to destroy the church and the Bible. Somewhat later, evolutionary theories found general acceptance largely through the writings of Charles Darwin (1809 – 1882). Bible students were affected by many rationalistic and evolutionary principles.

These principles had their strongest influence upon a new school of so-called historical-critical exegesis. Most of the historical-critical scholars of the 19th century were theological liberals. They often employed historical-critical methods to support their liberal views. In the minds of many, historical criticism and theological liberalism are inseparably connected. Unfortunately, they consider them almost synonymous terms.

But the historical-critical method of Bible study is perfectly proper and necessary in and of itself, even though, like all systems, it can be and is abused. In essence historical criticism asks such questions as: Who wrote the book? When? Why? Who were the original readers? What was their situation in life? What did the Word of God mean to them originally? (See Ch. 4 for more detailed discussion.)

Of course, many of the 19th-century historical critics had some preconceived ideas about the Christian religion and the Bible when they asked these questions. Their answers were often determined by their presuppositions rather than by careful historical study. They believed, for example, that the Christian religion was evolutionary and had moved from crude nature worship to advanced monotheism by the time of Isaiah and Micah. They dated complete books or, more commonly, portions of books by what they called the level of religious evolution that the contents represented. Julius Wellhausen (1844 – 1918) developed his theory of J, E, D, and P authors of parts of the Old Testament to support his evolutionary ideas.

Furthermore, many 19th-century Bible scholars did not believe that God intervened directly in the affairs of men. As rationalistic humanists they believed that the true Christian religion called for man to work out his own salvation. They denied the possibility of miracles and reinterpreted all the miracle stories of the Bible. Others believed that Jesus was the teacher of the good life but not the Son of God who had come down to earth to suffer and die for the sins of mankind. Such men felt called to "recover" the real Jesus of Nazareth so that His example might be held up for all men to imitate. They hoped that their Biblical studies would help in the establishment of lasting peace among people and nations.

The Biblical studies of many of these men had decidedly destructive effects upon the Bible. The point to remember here is that their liberal presuppositions controlled their Biblical interpretation much more noticeably than did the particular hermeneutical methods which they employed. Many of the conclusions reached by the 19th-century liberals have been disproved by careful and balanced study on the part of 20th-century exegetes.

But the ledger of the 19th-century Biblical study is by no means written exclusively in red ink. A galaxy of wise exegetes employed many of the same methods to produce a long list of valuable commentaries. These men combined a mastery of Biblical languages, grammar, and historical information with deep theological understanding. These commentators refused to emphasize historical and critical matters to the exclusion of the spiritual message of the book.

The presuppositions of these more sober men were in basic agreement with the traditional theological teachings of the Christian church, and their work has proved to be of lasting value. Outstanding men in this group were J. B. Lightfoot, B. F. Wescott, F. J. A. Hort, John A. Broadus, Theodor B. Zahn, Carl F. Keil, Franz Delitzsch, H. A. W. Meyer, John P. Lange, and F. Godet. Commentaries by these men are still being reprinted today and occupy honored positions in the libraries of many Christian pastors.

Biblical Studies in the 20th Century

Twentieth-century Biblical hermeneutics can be characterized by four adjectives: Christological, existential, ecumenical, and historical.

1. *Christological.* Almost every modern commentator of any importance bases his interpretation of the Bible on the conviction that Jesus Christ, the Son of God, is the absolute center of the Bible. They regard Him as the promised Messiah, the Fulfiller of the Old Testament, the center of all time and history, and the Savior of the world. This broad agreement represents one of the encouraging

developments of the current century. There is still room, however, for considerable further growth, for commentators are by no means agreed about what it means to say that the Christ is divine or the Son of God. Nor are they in agreement on the meaning of Jesus' suffering and death.

2. *Existential.* This is certainly the key word which describes the great majority of modern Bible interpreters. All employ a hermeneutical system which is existential to a greater or lesser degree. Broadly speaking, the word itself is related to "existence," which the philosopher might define as "the problem of human life or being."

Existentialist hermeneutics insists that the Bible must be interpreted as God's Word of judgment and deliverance to man in his total human situation. The interpreter's task, then, is to understand and explain the Word in such a way that both he and his hearer will experience a direct, personal meeting or confrontation with God. In such a "moment of existence," a person is called to make a decision of profound importance. For the existentialist, the historical accounts and the religious teachings of the Bible are of less importance than the profound, life-changing impact which God's Spirit can make upon the reader.

While there is an important truth in existentialist theory, these interpreters frequently operate with ideas about the Bible which seem strange to some Bible students. For example, they hold that the words of the Bible become the Word of God only if they have a profound, life-changing effect upon the reader. The name of a German theologian, Karl Barth, is often associated with this view.

Other Bible students in this group distinguish sharply between the form in which God's Word comes in the Bible and the content or *real meaning* of the Word. They believe that the Biblical record of a real Adam and Eve and a serpent which spoke belong to the form of the Word and can be discarded or ignored. The real meaning of Genesis 1 – 3 is that the human race is always rebellious and that its hope for the future rests solely upon God's good promises and mighty acts. This is a very simple illustration of "demythologizing" and brings to mind especially the name of Rudolf Bultmann.

3. *Ecumenical.* Twentieth-century Bible study can be described as ecumenical for two reasons: First, God's Spirit used renewed and intensive Biblical study to create and accelerate the ecumenical movement in this century. Newly discovered Biblical teachings about the old and new Israel, the kingdom of God, and the church sounded the call that led to new thinking about the nature of the church and its mission or task in the world. Second, 20th-century Bible study is ecumenical in the sense that it has led to widespread restudy of basic doctrines by members of all denominations. Bible students have discovered that in many cases the differences between denominations were matters of emphasis and word use rather than conflicting and necessarily divisive teachings. In both Biblical and doctrinal studies, scholars of the Roman Catholic Church did much of the pioneer work and produced books considered very helpful by scholars of many denominations.

4. *Historical.* Since the Reformation, Biblical studies have employed various historical methods and understandings, as will be indicated in more detail in Chapter 4. Here attention is called only to the hermeneutical use of the idea of "Salvation History" (German: *Heilsgeschichte* [heil's-geh-schich-teh]). This term suggests that the Bible must be read as a *history* of the great acts of God for the salvation of His chosen people in the Old and the New Testaments.

This hermeneutical principle that the Bible is salvation history has been widely accepted and provides the key idea for understanding many present-day commentaries and books on Biblical theology. Bible scholars holding this view insist that the Bible is the record of God's plan of salvation centered in Jesus Christ. It is therefore quite different from the sort of history reported in the daily newspapers or narrated in school and college texts. But it is nevertheless *history,* and this calls for the exegete to spend much of his time studying the *original* setting and meaning of Biblical words. Only after he has done this can the Bible student safely inquire about the present and future meaning of the passage.

Summary

This chapter has presented a brief but very important survey of the history of Bible study in the Christian church. Several hermeneutical principles used by New Testament writers to interpret the Old were discussed. The usefulness of the allegorical method and its weaknesses were analyzed in some detail because this method has been used widely by Christian Bible students. The important contributions of Martin Luther were reported briefly. The impact which the interpreter's views (his presuppositions) can have on his conclusions were studied in the systems of important exegetes of the 17th, 18th, and 19th centuries. Finally, the chief characteristics of 20th-century Bible study were described.

This chapter could not undertake a thorough examination and evaluation of each system mentioned. This was not its purpose. The rightness and wrongness or advantages and disadvantages of different hermeneutical principles used in the history of the church will become evident in the remaining chapters of this book.

1. From the New Testament give examples of the use of two different principles of hermeneutics in the interpretation of the Old Testament.

2. Define "allegory" in the sense in which Origen used it.

3. Why has allegorical exegesis always attracted followers?

4. Summarize Luther's views concerning the place of the Bible in the church.

5. What helpful and harmful roles may creeds and tradition play in the interpretation of Scripture?

6. How does John Calvin compare with Luther as an interpreter?

7. Define and illustrate what is meant by a presupposition. Give examples of some presuppositions which Bible students held in the 19th century and some still hold today.

8. In your own words, describe the dominant characteristics of Bible studies in the 20th century.

The next four chapters make up the heart of this text. They might best be read as a single unit. Cross-references will be made frequently from one part of a chapter to another chapter. However, despite their interrelation, the four units can be read and studied separately.

Chapter 3 will discuss the hermeneutical principles which flow from the fact that the Bible is the Word of God. They are called theological principles. Chapter 4 will discuss hermeneutical principles which are commonly employed to obtain the correct understanding of any literary work. Chapter 5 will then show how these basic principles are applied to the interpretation of major portions of the Old Testament, and Chapter 6 will illustrate this application to the New Testament.

Authorship and Authority of the Bible

The first truth which the believing Bible student accepts is that the Bible is uniquely the product of God's activity through the inspiration of His Spirit. The Bible makes this claim for itself in many passages, as was pointed out in Chapter 1. The Christian accepts these claims because God's Spirit, working in him through the Word of the Scriptures, convinces him of this source and nature of the Scriptures.

Because the Bible is the Word of God, it is not to be studied and interpreted in just the same way as other books. The hermeneutical principles considered in this chapter are related uniquely to the divine authorship of the Holy Scriptures and therefore also to its divine authority.

Purpose of the Bible

A clear understanding of the purpose of the Bible is basic to a proper system of Biblical interpretation. The purpose of the Bible is related to its nature, a topic that was treated in some detail in Chapter 1. There it was pointed out that the Bible is the Word of God. It was designed to reveal God's judgment and grace in the life of Israel; in the life, death, and resurrection of Jesus Christ; and in the early life and teachings of His church.

St. Paul spells out God's purpose for all this in 2 Tim. 3:14-17: "But as for you, continue in what you have learned and have firmly believed, knowing from whom you learned it and how from childhood you have been acquainted with the sacred writings which are able to *instruct you for salvation through faith in Christ Jesus.* All scripture is inspired by God and profitable for teaching, for reproof, for correction, and for training in righteousness, *that the man of God may be complete, equipped for every good work."*

In the quoted text the apostle mentions two inseparably connected purposes. The Bible is to instruct the reader for salvation through faith in Christ Jesus and is to enable the reader to become a completely equipped man of God. These results are of course dependent on the workings of the Holy Spirit, but God achieves them in large part as Christians read and study the Bible, and especially when they prayerfully search the Scriptures for the Word of truth and life called the Gospel.

The Timothy passage maintains that Biblical study is to be completely practical in nature. It is meant to edify the student and those whom he teaches. Bible study must lead to a growing understanding of God's grace, particularly as it was revealed in God's covenant relations with His people and in the person and work of His Son Jesus Christ, our Savior. Bible study must serve to nurture Christian faith, to help the learner live a Christian life, and to prepare him to welcome his Savior when He comes again.

Solus Christus

To accomplish this purpose, God speaks words of either judgment or grace, Law or Gospel, or both in every passage of the Bible. The proper understanding of these two concepts is essential to profitable Bible study. Luther identified the grace of God completely with the person and work of Jesus Christ. This identification led him to formulate a two-sided principle of Bible study. The first side of his principle is contained in his well-known statement that the Bible student must try to find Jesus Christ in every passage (German: *was Christum treibet*). The second aspect of his principle is too radical for many Bible students today, for it led him to question whether books like Esther and James, which in his opinion did not present Christ clearly if at all, should remain in the Bible!

Today the Bible student is taught a modified form of this first and very important principle of Martin Luther. He is taught to study each passage to find in it something about the judgment or the salvation which God has prepared for men. Naturally, this is done most easily in those passages which speak most clearly about His Son. Properly understood, this can be called the *solus Christus* (Christ alone) principle of Biblical hermeneutics.

Martin Luther expanded or amplified the *solus Christus* principle with three other "sola's": *sola gratia, sola fide,* and *sola scriptura.* While these "sola's" are not principles of interpretation, they provide important theological summaries and guidelines for proper interpretation.

With the phrase *sola gratia,* "by grace alone," Luther affirmed that the central teaching and unifying theme of the entire Bible is that God declares the sinner to be righteous solely and alone for the sake of Jesus Christ. Romans 4 and 5 contain a clear statement of this central truth. Abraham's faith that God would fulfill His promises was reckoned to him as righteousness (4:3). "Since, therefore, we are now justified by his [Christ's] blood, much more shall we be saved by him from the wrath of God." (5:9)

According to this principle any Bible interpretation which gives to man any credit for salvation is wrong or incomplete. Or to put this principle positively, the Bible student must not be satisfied until his interpretation magnifies the grace of God as the only hope of life and salvation.

Man can accept God's grace only by an act of faith or believing. And faith is also completely the work of the Holy Spirit. Luther summarized this important truth in the well-known phrase *sola fide,* meaning "through faith alone." By this phrase the Bible student judges as incorrect any interpretation which speaks favorably of man's works and efforts toward saving himself. This watchword, however, does not rule out man's participation in the will of God after he has come to faith. Like the first phrase, this second one encourages the Bible student to seek out those interpretations which focus attention on the activity of God—as Father, Son, or Holy Spirit.

Sola scriptura, "through Scripture alone," the third of Luther's Reformation "sola's," simply affirms that the

Bible tells Christians all they need to know about God's grace and saving faith and is the source and only *norm* or *standard* of Christian faith and life. *Sola scriptura* is, then, a statement about the primary importance of the Bible and its message of justification by grace through faith. In a sense, it underscores also the importance of *solus Christus* as a basic hermeneutical principle.

The Attitude of the Interpreter

Several references have been made to the motives, presuppositions, and spirit that the Bible student brings to his work. The student's attitude is obviously not a hermeneutical principle, but it will affect the outcome of his studies as deeply as the principles he uses. This study of Biblical interpretation assumes that the Bible student is a regenerated Christian, for only a Christian will accept most of the principles which are discussed in this chapter.

Law and Gospel

The believing Bible student expects that God will speak to him through His Word. God may speak words of Law—words that humble and terrify the reader, words that crush him because they expose his sinfulness and his spiritual nakedness before His Creator. Or God may speak words of Gospel—words that comfort, cheer, and encourage the frightened sinner because they speak of the great salvation which God has prepared in His Son Jesus Christ. Sometimes this idea of the double effect of the Word is turned into a hermeneutical principle which reads: Every passage of Scripture is either Law or Gospel.

But the Bible often cannot be catalogued neatly as either Law or Gospel. One might debate, for example, whether the story of the crucifixion is Law or Gospel. It is both, for it portrays vividly the anger of God against sin as well as His boundless love for the sinner. Again and again the Bible student will find that a passage which he understood as Law one day will speak Gospel another day. In short, the Bible student is reminded that his study and explanation of a Biblical text is wrong or incomplete until he has been addressed by His Creator in terms of both Law and Gospel.

The Work of the Spirit

It is necessary that the Bible student be a believing Christian so that his mind and heart will be open to the discernment and direction of the Holy Spirit. Jesus promised that His Spirit would lead His followers into all truth. Only the Spirit of God in the spirit of the Bible student will lead him to the true and full meaning of a passage. The Bible student therefore must pray for the illumination of the Spirit as did the psalmist who wrote, "Open my eyes, that I may behold wondrous things out of Thy law." (Ps. 119:18)

This promise has frequently been misunderstood and misapplied. Some have used it as an excuse for avoiding the hard work which Biblical interpretation demands. In place of studying, such people often claim that they receive an interpretation of a Biblical passage directly from God. Others will say that they can ignore all the basic principles of interpretation because they have received a direct personal interpretation. When some persons once made this claim to Martin Luther, he told them to perform a miracle to prove that they were so closely affiliated with the Holy Spirit!

Pietist Christians sometimes err in this respect by claiming that their subjective personal feelings or convictions are proof that their interpretations have come from the Holy Spirit. Bible study clubs or groups can make this mistake, too, when a member has a "hunch" or a "feeling" about what a passage means and the other members regard such a "hunch" as a direct message from God.

The proper attitude of the interpreter can be summarized in the words which the Lord caused Isaiah to record: "But this is the man to whom I will look, he that is humble and contrite in spirit and trembles at My Word." (Is. 66:2)

Scripture Interprets Itself

Christian theologians have always defended the principle that the Bible is clear and that its meanings can be understood by even the simplest Christians. But today this principle is under heavy fire. In the opinion of many it requires a great deal of intelligence and learning to interpret the Scriptures correctly. It seems that the Bible student must know history, archaeology, philosophy, and linguistics as well as Hebrew, Greek, and Aramaic. The average Bible student is inclined to throw up his hands in dismay and to leave the field of Biblical interpretation to seminary professors.

But it will be a sad day for the church if Biblical interpretation ever becomes the monopoly of the highly trained exegete. Fortunately this situation need not come to pass, for Scripture in general *is* clear and its teachings can be understood by the simplest Christian. Isn't this, however, an apparent contradiction? On the one hand we maintain the principle of the sufficient clarity of Scripture while on the other hand we insist that a system of hermeneutics is necessary and that learned exegetes are very important!

The answer to this paradox lies in the proper understanding of the clarity of the Scripture. In the first place, the principle of clarity is simply this: Any regenerated Christian should be able to read or hear the Bible in such a way that he can learn what he needs to know about

God's plan of salvation and about His will for human life. The passages which are usually quoted in defense of the clarity of Scripture (for example, Ps. 119:105, 130; 2 Peter 1:19) insist only that the Word of God gives light to the simple.

The "clarity" passages must be balanced by those passages which enjoin careful and diligent study (Deut. 17: 19; 2 Chron. 17:9; Is. 2:3; Acts 17:11). The apostle Peter warns the readers of Paul's epistles that "there are some things in them hard to understand, which the ignorant and unstable twist to their own destruction, as they do the other Scriptures." (2 Peter 3:16. See also v. 18; Heb. 6:1-3; 1 Peter 1:10-12.)

Thus, Scripture itself speaks both of its clarity and of the difficult passages which require study. The principle that the Gospel, the story of God's salvation through Jesus Christ, is taught so clearly in Scripture that it can be understood by any believing Christian is the basic hermeneutical principle which this section is stressing.

The clarity principle can be applied, in the second place, to a larger group of passages which are clear in their meaning, even though they may teach more than the plain simple Gospel of Jesus Christ in the narrow sense. Biblical interpreters employ the rule that everything essential to man's redemption and to his new life in Christ is clearly taught somewhere in the Scripture (Latin: *locus classicus* [low'-kus klass-e-kus]).

The Analogy of Faith

The use of the analogy of faith plays an important role in Biblical interpretation. "Analogy" means the correct relation or agreement between two or more items. "Faith" in this phrase means the body of Christian doctrine, that which Christians confess, rather than faith in the more frequent Pauline sense of the believer's confident relationship to God through Jesus Christ. Thus "analogy of faith" means that the teachings drawn from Bible passages should be in agreement with the creedal and confessional statements of the Christian church, which in turn are based on the clear passages of Scripture.

Scholars today remind us that Luther limited the analogy of faith to the Gospel, that is, the good news that God was in Christ, reconciling the world unto Himself. The application of the analogy of faith meant for Luther that no interpretation could be correct if it resulted in a teaching which in any way contradicted this central message of the Bible.

In the post-Reformation period, the term came to be used to describe all the chief doctrines of the church, that is, those doctrines which are emphasized in most catechisms and in courses for church membership. Theologians prepared catalogs of the clear passages in which these basic teachings were clearly set forth. These catalogs, in turn, were used to control the interpretation of unclear or debatable passages. The analogy-of-faith principle reminds the Bible student to explain less clear passages by relating them, point by point, to the standard clear passages which treat of the same subject.

Of course there are many unclear passages in the Bible which are not directly related to a clear one, and so this principle does not help in every case; but it is a valuable principle nevertheless. For example, the truth that not everyone will be saved is clearly revealed in Matt. 24: 36-51. This doctrine ought not, therefore, be based primarily upon the curious reference in Revelation to the 144,000 saved. Likewise 1 Cor. 15:29 is a difficult and unclear passage and should not be used for a doctrine of proxy baptism, as is practiced, for example, by the Mormon Church. There are clearer passages on baptism.

The history of Bible study shows that Christians are often inclined to abuse this principle. This abuse can take place, for example, when the Christian concentrates on a relatively small number of clear, basic passages and neglects the study of the rest of the Bible. Or, more seriously, the Christian may concentrate on the catechism or books which have been written about the clear passages and may never really open his Bible for further study.

The principle of the analogy of faith can also be abused by theologians who insist that no two passages of Scripture are correctly interpreted if they seem to state contradictory truths. For example, some will argue that, since Scrpture teaches Christ's bodily ascension into heaven, therefore His body cannot be present in any real corporeal sense in the Sacrament of the Altar. But Scripture affirms the real (we say sacramental) presence of the Lord's body and blood in the Sacrament as clearly as it teaches that Christ ascended heavenward bodily. When two passages appear to contradict each other, the student of Scripture must interpret both passages in keeping with good hermeneutical principles and then, if he cannot resolve the disagreement, he must permit it to stand.

The Analogy of Scripture

This leads to another important principle, namely that the Scriptures do not contradict themselves. It is better to limit this principle to the analogy of faith, as described above, than to make it a blanket principle which one can apply literally to each and every verse. Scripture does contain various types of contradictory statements. Some point out, for example, that Law and Gospel are contradictory in their message. Jesus often spoke the truth in paradoxes. Paul and James make opposing statements, both of which are true when rightly understood. In some cases, historical facts are reported in differing versions. (Compare Gal. 3:17 with Gen. 12:4, 21:5, 25:26, and 47:9; Gen. 28:18f with 35:15; 2 Sam. 24:9 with 1 Chron. 21:5; 1 Kings 4:26 with 2 Chron. 9:25; Matt. 20:29 with Luke 18:35; etc.)

The important theological principle to remember in connection with the analogy of Scripture is that God's Word cannot contradict itself in accomplishing its stated purpose, that of instructing men for salvation through faith which is in Christ Jesus. Every word of Scripture is true and reliable. In a case where contradictions may exist in fact or may seem to exist because of an inadequate interpretation, the Christian student looks for the truth of the Spirit in both the "Yes" and the "No."

For example, at one time Jesus said, "Do not think that I have come to bring peace on earth; I have not come to bring peace, but a sword" (Matt. 10:34). At another time He said, "Peace I leave with you; My peace I give to you" (John 14:27). Paul wrote, "We hold that a man is justified by faith apart from works of law" (Rom. 3:28). But James wrote by the inspiration of the same Spirit of God, "You see that a man is justified by works and not by faith alone" (James 2:24). All are the words of God.

Progressive Revelation

Another important consideration when discussing contradictions in the Bible is that of progressive, or cumulative, revelation. Both adjectives have been misused and have come to have a bad reputation, but they can be used rightly to describe a basic characteristic of Scripture. Some scholars have used the idea of "progressive revelation" to express their belief that the Biblical religion is a completely evolutionary development which gradually progressed from purest paganism to a high understanding of monotheism. The term is not used in that rational and humanistic sense in this book. In this study it refers to the fact that God revealed spiritual truths to man in partial but adequate fashion before the time of Christ (Gal. 4:1-7; Heb. 1:1-2). Because Jesus Christ ful-filled the Old Testament revelation of God, in a very real sense the New Testament is a *new* and *fuller* revelation.

This fact helps us to understand many passages in the New Testament which seem to contradict or even cancel teachings found in Old Testament passages. Thus in Mark 10:2-9 Jesus cancelled a law found in Deut. 24:1-4 and then showed why the old regulation had to be changed in view of His deeper, more spiritual interpretation. In Galatians St. Paul speaks of Old Testament law as the custodian of God's people "until Christ came" (Gal. 3:24-25), but Paul saw the greater light and glory in the grace of Jesus Christ. Our Lord's remarks about Old Testament law in the Sermon on the Mount reflect this same attitude.

But the Bible student must also remember that there is a progression or accumulation within the Old Testament revelation. The prophecies of the coming Savior became more clear and precise as the history of Israel moved along. (See the fuller discussion of Messianic prophecy in Chapter 5.) The Israelites also seem to have gained clearer understandings of the nature of God's will for human life. The polygamy of Solomon's day was not practiced by later monarchs. The "eye for an eye" legislation is replaced by Micah's fine summary principle, "to do justice and to love kindness" (Micah 6:8), and so forth.

The Relationship Between the Testaments

The question of the relationship between the Testaments may be explored in somewhat greater detail. In this matter three mistakes have been commonly made by Bible students. One group (the Gnostics in the first Christian centuries and some present-day interpreters) has argued that the Old Testament has little or nothing to say to the Christian church. Another group (legalistic) has argued that the two Testaments are of equal importance and authority, thus denying the newness that Jesus Christ brought. A third group (Justin Martyr [flourished A. D. 150] and some present-day catechisms) has argued that only certain passages from the Old Testament have value for the Christian today. Usually this group will pick out the Messianic prophecies and a few moral stories.

The relationship is well expressed in a little couplet that, translated into English, goes like this:

The new is in the old concealed;
The old is in the new revealed.

This suggests that the Bible student as a general rule must look to New Testament passages for final answers. Thus Old Testament rules about eating and days of worship properly give way to New Testament teachings on these subjects. But this couplet also underscores the importance of studying the Old Testament. Our Lord's life and work make much greater sense when studied in the light of the Old Testament. The letter to the Hebrews, St. Paul's letters to the Galatians and the Romans, and the Book of Revelation, among others, can be correctly understood only by a student who is acquainted with the Old Testament.

The Intended Meaning

A widely discussed principle of Bible study today is that the Holy Spirit intended the words and statements of the Bible to have only one meaning. The allegorists rejected this principle and found two or more meanings in every word. They made the Bible say what they wanted it to say. Today this principle comes to bear in a discussion of the literal and the figurative meanings of Scripture passages.

It should be noted in passing that this principle applies to any literary production. The writer writes in order to be understood, and, unless there are good reasons to the contrary, he uses words in such a way that the readers will get at least the general drift of what is in his mind.

But today philosophers remind us that the precise and intended meanings of words are much more difficult to "nail down" than most of us realize. To test this idea, simply ask five people to define the common Biblical word "holy." You will very likely receive five different definitions, especially if you insist that people give you more than a vague generality. Probably no one of the five definitions will correspond exactly with your own.

"Words," a famous fiction character once said, "mean exactly what I want them to mean; nothing more and nothing less." This is an overstatement, but it does point to a truth that the Bible student should keep in mind. He must learn to define words with reference to the total thought system of the writer. The distinction between literal and figurative meanings also must be considered in the light of this concept of the function of word meanings.

With this thought in mind, the Bible student also recognizes that it is not always easy to determine with a clearcut line whether a particular Bible passage was meant to have a *literal* meaning or whether God intended us to understand it *figuratively*. Is it, for example, prophetic or parabolic in form? The rule of thumb to follow in deciding whether to understand a passage literally or figuratively is that we must assume the "normal and natural" meaning of words unless the writer signals to us that he is using them in a different, or figurative, sense. For example, the Bible reader will assume that "lamb" means a young sheep (Gen. 22:7-8) unless the writer somehow indicates a different intended meaning, as is evident in John 1:29-36 and Rev. 22:1-3.

But when a writer signals a "nonliteral" meaning, a figurative meaning, then the simple concrete meaning of words may be far from the truth. While some of the signals of language are easy to catch, others can be recognized only after careful study and practice. Clearly, "cows of Bashan" in Amos 4:1 refers to the wives of greedy men rather than to the bovines for which this region was famous. Some of the more easily recognized forms of figurative language are the parable and the apocalyptic vision.

There are many other literary forms used by Biblical writers which are not so easily recognized by the Bible student. One book on Biblical interpretation devotes 150 of its 400 pages to the discussion of literary forms and figures of speech in the Bible, but it uses only 24 of these pages to explain the relatively few discussed in this chapter!

The metaphor is a common figure of speech in which the writer describes one thing in terms of something else that may perhaps be better known to the readers (Luke 8: 21; 22:31-34). Another form of metaphor is used when God is described in terms of human experience and emotions. These metaphors are called anthropomorphisms (Deut. 4:34; 5:15; Ps. 44:3), or anthropopathisms (Ps. 95: 10; Heb. 3:10; Gen. 6:1-8). In metonymy the name of one thing is used for another because the two are commonly associated. Thus "Moses" in the New Testament sometimes means the first five books of the Bible. (Luke 16:29)

Scholars are continually identifying other literary forms in the Scriptures, especially in the Old Testament. New discoveries of pagan literature often make these identifications possible. One of the most vexing questions in Biblical interpretation today centers around one such type of literary form called "myth." In pagan literature "myth" means a story, either fictional or historically factual, which is told for the purpose of presenting a truth that, in the narrator's judgment, is basic and unchanging. In this sense the poems of Homer are filled with myths about the gods. In the interpretation of these stories the emphasis must be placed upon the truth the poet wished to communicate rather than upon the details of the gods' habits or conduct.

Many Bible scholars are convinced that portions of the Bible are mythical in this literary sense of the word. Genesis 1 – 11 is often cited as an example. They believe that

God's purpose in inspiring these narratives was to teach fundamental truths about Himself and about man rather than detailed facts of actual happenings. Other Bible scholars argue that if parts of Genesis 1—11 and other portions of the Bible are mythical and perhaps not historical in every detail, then Christians cannot be certain that any of the recorded events in the Bible are historically true, including the accounts of our Lord's death and resurrection.

It may help the reader to deal with this problem if he keeps in mind, first, that God's Spirit often used nonhistorical materials in historical form in order to teach fundamental truths. The parable of the Good Samaritan is an example. Second, however, there must be clear indications or cues that point to the possibility of its mythical character before the interpreter may consider a passage to be nonhistorical. The passion narratives completely lack such "myth signals," and so the reader need not take seriously the argument that if there is myth anywhere in the Bible, then perhaps it is all mythical. Remember, too, that "mythical" stories may be historically factual, in whole or part.

The correct identification of the literary form or figure of speech is quite important both for proper interpretation and for the preservation of the principle that the intended meaning of each Biblical word or passage is single. Even when a word is used in a figure of speech, its meaning is still a single meaning. When Jesus figuratively calls Himself the Door (John 10:7), the word "door" means only "a passage or a means of access." Failure to understand this principle or to use it correctly is one of the commonest mistakes made by both amateur and professional Bible interpreters.

Summary

This chapter contains a discussion of the more important hermeneutical principles related to the Bible's unique nature. Divine inspiration was stressed, as was also the importance of understanding the purpose for which the Bible was given. The centrality of Jesus Christ and the Gospel and their relationship to Bible study was underscored. The proper attitude of the interpreter was described. This was followed by an explanation of the principles that the Bible is clear, that it interprets itself, that the Scriptures do not contradict themselves, and that the meaning intended by God is always a single one. The chapter closed by stressing the importance of recognizing literary forms and figures of speech.

TO HELP YOU REVIEW

1. What does St. Paul say about the purpose of Scripture in 2 Tim. 3:14-16? What does the passage contribute to a good system of interpretation?

2. What is the main message of the Bible? How is this central message related to Luther's *sola gratia* (solely by grace), *sola fide* (solely by faith), and *sola scriptura* (solely by Scripture)?

3. What role does the Holy Spirit play in Bible interpretation? How do some people misinterpret the doctrine of the Holy Spirit as teacher?

4. Why is the attitude of the interpreter important? How would you define a proper attitude?

5. What is meant by the statement that "Scripture interprets itself"? In what sense can this rule be misunderstood?

6. Define "analogy of faith" and show its role in the interpretation of the Bible.

7. Define "analogy of Scripture" and show why this principle is important in interpretation.

8. What is meant by the rule, "The intended meaning of a Scripture passage is single"? How did the medieval allegorists ignore this principle?

This chapter will discuss *general* principles of Biblical interpretation. They are called "general principles" because they are used also in getting at the meaning of *non-*Biblical literary works. The previous chapter dealt with principles based upon the unique nature and purpose of the Bible. The general principles will be considered in reference to their use in Bible study.

The Text

The first step in the interpretation of any literary document is to make sure that one has the actual words of the author. Most ancient literary productions have been copied and recopied so often that there are many variations in the text. This is true also of the ancient Biblical writings. There are hundreds of thousands of variant readings in the thousands of ancient Biblical manuscripts which are now available.

In spite of countless variants, Bible scholars are quite confident of the correct text in the vast majority of verses. They reach their conclusions by the careful use of the discipline of textual criticism. The method cannot be discussed in this small book, but it is enough to note that the method is scientific and reliable.

In some cases, textual critics are still debating as to the original words. Newer translations indicate by footnotes the chief passages where textual critics are not in unanimous agreement. See, for example, the Revised Standard Version (Matt. 12:46-48; 21:43-45; Rom. 5:1-2) and the New English Bible (Matt. 12:41 [note the conclusion of the NEB editors]; Acts 5:30; Gal. 2:4-5). The Bible reader who is not skilled in textual criticism can rely on the standard English texts.

Literary Principles of Interpretation

Grammar and Style

The Bible student who works in the original Biblical languages spends much of his time in the study and analysis of grammar. Grammar itself supplies the rules or principles according to which a writer relates words and various parts of the sentence to each other so that his readers will understand his point. The Greek language is particularly delicate in grammatical distinctions. Hebrew, the language of the Old Testament, is not as refined; it is geared to the Oriental or Eastern way of thinking, which is more sensitive to the mysteries and meanings of the heart and less precise intellectually.

As in the case of textual criticism, the student who works with the English Bible can rely upon the standard, generally used English translations. But he must remember that the exact translation of Hebrew and Greek grammatical constructions and expressions into English (or any other language) is not easy. Frequently a comparison of several English translations will show how good translators have translated the same original into very different sentences in their efforts to capture the sense of the original. For example, 1 Cor. 10:17 can be translated: "Because there is one loaf, we, many as we are, are one body"; or: "For we, many as we are, are one loaf, one body"; or "Because there is one bread, we who are many are one body, for we all partake of the one bread."

A comparative study of translations may reveal different meanings, in which case the student must check a commentary which discusses the original text. The original meaning and intent of a given text, it must be repeated, is also determined by much more than formal grammar. Living language often communicates its meanings through a style which is not subject to formal grammar and grammatical analysis. This is why a "literal" translation may fail completely to communicate what was said originally.

Word Usage

A good portion of the Bible student's time will be spent in the study of individual words, for they are boxcars that carry much of the freight of the divinely intended meaning. Again the most important word study is carried on by those who work directly with the Biblical languages, but there are several things which the English Bible student can do in the study of the words in an English version.

In the first place, we must remember that many of the words in the King James Version have changed in meaning over the centuries and that many of the words mean something different to us than they did to the original hearers. "Bishop," the Greek word *episcopos,* is an example. In the New Testament the word refers to overseers or elders who performed the pastoral functions of the local congregation. Today it often brings to mind a picture of one who wields considerable religious authority and power over a group of congregations.

Furthermore, the Bible student will do well to check various English translations to acquaint himself with the differing shades of meaning that Bible scholars see in the original Greek or Hebrew word. He can also become familiar with the Biblical wordbooks described in Chapter 7.

Most important, the Bible student can write his own dictionary of meanings as he studies the Bible over the years. The process is painstaking but valuable, and the technique is quite simple.

Take the important word "kingdom" as an example. Begin with a good concordance which lists the verses in which the word is found. Select the passages which appear to be most helpful. Write the key phrase on the left side of a sheet of paper and your own brief summary of its meaning on the right side. Then prepare a brief summary statement (50 – 500 words) of the meaning of the word "kingdom" in the Bible on the basis of your own analysis. It's a good idea to group the passages according to individual authors, for often one author's usage of a word will differ from that of another.

Context

Even though the study of grammar and individual words is a prerequisite in determining an intended meaning, the true meaning can be gained only by studying the words, phrases, verses, or sections in their settings and in relation to what comes before and what follows. This is called the context principle. Considerable violence can be done to the intended meaning of a writer or speaker by quoting his words out of their original context.

It may be helpful to think of four circles of context which the Bible student must consider. The first circle is that of the immediately preceding and following verses. Newer translations break the Biblical material into paragraphs to indicate the natural thought units of the author. This is helpful, for the chapter and verse numberings often confuse rather than help the Bible student. For example, the study of Isaiah 53 really ought to begin with 52:13; the interpretation of Gen. 3:15 requires looking back all the way to 2:1; and so forth.

The second contextual circle is that of the entire book or letter in which the passage appears. If James 2:18-24 is taken out of the context of the book, it seems to teach salvation by works, which is in direct contradiction to many other clear Biblical statements. But a study of the book as a whole makes it apparent that James is concerned with a misunderstanding of faith and is showing that faith in Jesus must be applied to all the relationships and experiences of the believer.

A third circle of context embraces all books written by a given writer. To thoroughly understand St. Paul's thought in Romans 9 — 11, which some Biblical commentators feel is the heart and center of the epistle, the Bible student must aquaint himself with the apostle's thought about God's purposes in history, the fate of Israel, and the newness of life brought by Jesus Christ. He gains these insights by reading widely in all Paul's letters.

The fourth circle is that of the entire Bible. Here the student brings to bear what he knows about God's purpose in giving the Bible, the chief themes in the Bible, the concept of Gospel, the analogies of faith and of Scripture, and so forth.

Cross-References

The use of Biblical cross-references also belongs to a discussion of the circle of contexts. Cross-references are selected by Biblical editors on several principles. Some will give a cross-reference to a passage if the same key word occurs in it. Some may give a cross-reference to a passage which treats of the same general subject, even though the same word does not appear. Some will give cross-references to passages which in their judgment confirm their own interpretation. Cross-references, like word studies, serve to add light to the study of a passage.

The importance of historical considerations in the interpretation of Scripture has come to be increasingly recognized since the Reformation. Today they are commonly acknowledged.

Historical principles are of two general types. One set answers questions as to when, where, why, to whom, and by whom a book was written. A second set addresses to the Bible the kind of questions which historians in general ask and attempt to answer. It includes questions of cause and effect (What really caused the wind to become calm? Why did the people react as they did?), the possibility and nature of divine intervention in human affairs, the meaning that the event had for people at the time it happened, the nature of history writing, etc. No one questions the value of the first set of questions. It is the use of the second set that has disturbed many Christians. The use of the first set of historical-critical principles calls for a careful study of the material that casts light on questions of authorship and original readers. The Bible student wants to know, if at all possible, who wrote the book. For many of the history books of the Old Testament (1 and 2 Samuel; 1 and 2 Kings; 1 and 2 Chronicles; Ezra; Nehemiah; Esther; Job) and for at least one of the books of the New Testament (Hebrews) this question cannot be answered. In such cases the best that one can do is to reconstruct the sort of person or group of people who might have produced the book. (For example, Luther's intelligent guess was that Apollos might have written the letter to the Hebrews.)

History and Culture

Next it is important to reconstruct the situation and the needs of the original readers or hearers as fully and accurately as possible. This is a crucial step, for the Bible student's first task is to learn what the words meant "then and there" to the first readers. For some of the prophetic books and many of Paul's letters this is quite easy to do, largely because of information supplied by the book itself.

In reconstructing the original situation, the Bible student will be greatly aided by some knowledge of Biblical geography, history, and culture. The student is advised to read a book or two on each of these topics rather than to try to pick up scattered bits of information from commentaries.

The importance of some knowledge of the culture of a period in history can readily be demonstated. When Paul wrote of Jesus as one in whom all the fulness of the Godhead dwells bodily (Col. 1:19—2:9), his words had a greater impact on the Colossians than they probably have on most readers today. The Greek word for "fulness" was a technical word used by certain religious teachers of that Greek world to describe their utterly unreachable god whom they conceived as having absolutely no connection with corrupt human flesh. In effect Paul was saying: "God has made His complete fulness, His power and person, available to everyone by coming into the world incarnate (in the flesh of Jesus of Nazareth)." The spiritual riches of this passage are uncovered most fully by one who has some knowledge of Colossian culture and religion.

Historical Interpretation

Establishing the "then and there" meaning is often difficult work, as the preceding paragraphs have indicated. Sometimes, frankly, we cannot be sure we have caught the real "then and there" meaning because the text itself may not be clear or our knowledge of history and culture may not be adequate. But this step represents the essential control by which the valid present-day application of the passage is established.

The Bible student is always tempted to take just "a one-eyed squint" at a passage before deciding its meaning for his life. For example, John the Baptizer said, "He must increase, but I must decrease" (John 3:30). Bernard Ramm maintains that the strict interpretation of this passage (the "then and there" meaning) is that John must decrease in *popularity* with the people as our Lord increases in *popularity*. Only with this awareness may we apply this to our lives in saying, for example, that our plans, programs, and self-interests must give way in consecration to Christ.

Psalm 110 is often used to illustrate this same principle. This psalm is so remarkably similar to poems which were written to be read or sung at the coronation of Eastern rulers that Bible scholars are convinced that Psalm 110 is somehow related to this use. It might, then, be viewed as a call to the Israelites to give thanks because God had kept His promises to them and had preserved their religious and national independence and strength through the office of the king, an office which was again being filled by another candidate chosen and anointed by God. This probably was the "then and there" meaning of Psalm 110 for most of those who first heard it.

However, many passages in the Psalms and in other Old Testament books speak glowingly of the coming King and the coming kingdom which God would establish in the future. These prophecies center in the idea of a great anointed (anointed — Messiah) King, who would bring to a climax the good work of all previous kings and who would reign in glory over Israel. In its use of Psalm 110 the New Testament makes clear that the promise of the coming King reached its greatest and its final fulfillment in Him who was descended from the tribe of David, who conquered death and hell, and who now reigns over His people in Messianic glory.

Interpretation and Application

As has been suggested, there is an important distinction

between interpretation and application. Interpretation establishes the meaning which God's Spirit intended to convey through a passage. This meaning can only be single (see Chapter 3). In the preceding section it was noted that the *original* meanings of some passages no longer speak directly to later generations (see again, for example, 1 Cor. 10), and that therefore an *application* of the meaning must be made. (Compare John 3:30.)

As customs, understandings, and needs change, there may be *several* applications of a specific passage in subsequent periods of the church's history. This is especially true of many of the inspiring poetic passages in the Psalms. However, the Bible student is cautioned to remember that an application which he makes must not contradict the divinely intended meaning of a passage.

For example, the application of 1 Cor. 11:2-10 is not a universal law that women must wear hats in church. In the past Paul's words were thus interpreted. However, Paul's instructions find their validity in the customs of his day, when women were considered immodest if they appeared in public with their heads uncovered.

The Nature of History Writing

In this section on historical considerations related to interpretation, a few words must be said about the complex subject of how authors record history. In general, Bible scholars today are agreed that Biblical writers wrote their historical sections very much like noninspired historians of their time wrote. Several characteristics of history writing are noteworthy.

The first is the fact that all Biblical writers of history had written or oral sources upon which they based their own inspired accounts. Luke 1:1-4 is a clear statement of this fact. (See also 2 Sam. 1:18; 1 Kings 14:19; 2 Kings 8:23; 2 Chron. 9:29.) A comparison of passages in Exodus and Deuteronomy will reveal that Deuteronomy has a somewhat different emphasis than Exodus, to meet the needs of the people for whom each book was written. (Note for example, the similarities and differences between Ex. 20:8-12 and Deut. 5:12-16 or between Ex. 23:14-17 and Deut. 16:1-17.)

A comparative study of the gospels indicates that each writer chose his narratives from a larger store of records and sayings of Jesus. A look at the table of contents of the first three gospels shows that the inspired writers occasionally placed the same narratives in a different order. It is important to study these differences in the treatment of the same material, for the patterns of similarities and differences may provide an important clue to the proper interpretation of the section or the book.

This leads to the second characteristic of all history writing, namely that the historians' own feelings and interests show up in their books and that all of them write history to develop a point of view. This is as true of writers inspired by God as it is of regular historians. For example, it has long been recognized that each of the gospel writers was presenting his own particular view of Jesus Christ and His Gospel. Matthew wrote to show that Jesus is the fulfillment of the Old Testament, while Luke emphasized that Jesus is the world's Savior and the Friend of the outcast and downtrodden. John was inspired by God to set forth clearly that Jesus is the Son of God. Because of its special purpose the content and emphasis of his gospel is quite different from that of the others.

The recognition of each writer's point of view and purpose by no means suggests that their varying accounts are contradictory or filled with error. It rather accents the truth that it is impossible for any historian to describe an event or action in a completely impersonal manner, without seeing the matter through his particular and limited viewpoint. Apparently the inspiring Spirit did not avoid this basic law of human behavior.

General Principles of Biblical Interpretation

The Bible student will therefore find it necessary to acquaint himself with the theological theme and general purpose of a book, even a "history" book, if his interpretation is to be correct. As was pointed out in Chapter 1, this understanding of human characteristics of the writer and his book does not call the inspiration of God into question. A more extended discussion of the second set of historical principles would involve the reader in profound philosophical questions on which not even the scholars are presently in agreement.

Summary

This chapter discussed principles of interpretation which are commonly used in the study of any literary work and applied these principles specifically to Bible study. The necessity and nature of textual criticism were indicated. Then the difficulty of translating Hebrew and Greek into English was illustrated. This was followed by a discussion of interpretation on the basis of four circles of context. The chapter also concerned itself with the importance of historical principles in *literary* interpretation. The importance of deciding when, where, why, by whom, and to whom a book was written was discussed in some detail. The necessity of establishing the "then and there" meaning and of distinguishing between this meaning and a possible variety of applications was also pointed out. Finally, something was said about the nature of Biblical *history* writing, and the use of source material by inspired writers was acknowledged.

TO HELP YOU REVIEW

1. Distinguish between theological principles (Ch. 3) and general principles (Ch. 4).

2. Why is an understanding of basic rules of grammar important in Biblical interpretation?

3. Summarize the steps by which a word study might be carried out.

4. Explain what is meant by the four circles of context.

5. Distinguish between the two types of historical questions that Bible students are asking about the Bible today.

6. What is meant by the "then and there" meaning of a passage? How does this "then and there" rule help to determine the intended meaning of the text?

7. Distinguish precisely between meaning and application as the terms are used in this book. What is the principle of the "single meaning"?

8. Summarize the important points about the nature of historical writing in the Scripture. How will this knowledge help the interpreter?

We now proceed to a discussion of some of the specific guidelines for interpreting the major portions of the Old Testament. Chapters 3 and 4 dealt with "theological" and "general" principles which are applicable to both Testaments. The use of these principles will be assumed in this chapter.

The distinction between Chapters 5 and 6 does not suggest a sharp division between the Old and the New Testaments. Nor does it imply that a separate set of principles is used for the interpretation of each Testament. The separate discussions are designed to help the reader apply the principles he has already studied, as well as several new principles, to the interpretation of larger sections of material in each of the Testaments.

The Basic Purpose of the Old Testament

The Old Testament is the story of the great acts of judgment and deliverance by which God chose for Himself a people, the Children of Israel, and then kept them as His chosen nation despite their sinfulness and repeated rebellion in order that His covenant promises to the whole human race might be preserved and fulfilled in the

Son of David, the Christ, who became the Son of Man, Jesus, the Savior of the world. This theological purpose marks all the Old Testament books.

Ex. 19:1-6 is a key passage for a proper interpretation of the Old Testament. It reads in part as follows: "Now therefore, if you will obey My voice and keep My covenant, you shall be My own possession among all peoples; for all the earth is Mine, and you shall be to Me a kingdom of priests and a holy nation."

It is noteworthy that St. Peter summarizes God's purposes for His church, the followers of Christ, in almost the same words in the New Testament: "But you are a chosen race, a royal priesthood, a holy nation, God's own people, that you may declare the wonderful deeds of Him who called you out of darkness into His marvelous light" (1 Peter 2:9). The passage from Peter reminds us again of the theological unity of the two Testaments and of the importance of studying them together.

Interpreting Historical Passages

The two passages quoted above indicate two things which the Bible student needs to keep in mind. The first is that the historical books (and the historical sections in the nonhistorical books) contain much theological information. They tell the reader a great deal about what God is like, about His purposes in the world, and about the responses which God expects from His creatures. As one studies history in the Old Testament, God is encountered in a very real and personal sense. The reader comes to know and appreciate God's faithfulness to all His promises. He comes to understand God's anger at sin and His great love and mercy toward the sinner. He comes to recognize that Old Testament history was on the move and that God was moving it constantly toward the time of the New Testament. The reader also senses that the history of

Israel is his personal history too. It is not something which happened only in the long-forgotten past.

The second basic insight to be gained from the two passages is that God's overall purpose in history is to preserve at all times and in all places a chosen people in whose midst He dwells and who in turn show forth His praises. In other words, the Bible's message was directed toward God's people as they lived in relationship to other people and was concerned with keeping God's people in a covenant and faith relation with Him. We who study the Bible today are, so to speak, in touch with God's people of the past.

How Old Testament History Was Written

In Chapter 4 the nature of Biblical history writing was discussed. It was pointed out that there is no such thing as written history that describes an event with such complete fulness that the reader thereby knows everything that happened exactly as it happened. A cursory study of two descriptions of the reign of King Hezekiah will illustrate this important point. His career is described in 2 Kings 18—20 and in 2 Chronicles 29—32. In 2 Chronicles the emphasis is placed upon Hezekiah's reform of the Israelite worship, the reopening of the temple, the prohibition of idol worship, and the reform of temple finances. The story of the destruction of the Assyrians is told rather briefly in 22 verses. In the account in 2 Kings, one verse is devoted to Hezekiah's reform program, while the Assyrian invasion is related in considerable detail in chapters 18:13—19:37.

Quite evidently each writer was teaching a different lesson by selecting and emphasizing different events from the king's life. The chronicler apparently was very much interested in liturgical reform, while the author of 2 Kings may have wished to emphasize a miraculous act of God to comfort and encourage his readers in the face of other troubles. The student of the Scriptures ought to acquaint himself with the theological point of view of a particular historical book in order to interpret portions of the book correctly.

This understanding of Biblical history writing is very important, but the Bible student is cautioned against wrong conclusions which are often drawn from this human, individual aspect of any part of the Bible. For example, some will point to the illustration of Hezekiah's two biographies and argue that both 2 Kings and 2 Chronicles contain accounts which the authors made up to suit their respective point of view. But this conclusion does not follow from the fact that each writer was obviously selective in writing the record of the king's reign. Nor does it follow that there are errors in one account or the other simply because they are not identical.

The important principle is that the student of the Bible needs to have a clear understanding of why each book was written if he is to study it intelligently and profitably. This information is available in many books of Biblical introduction, which serve to acquaint students with the purpose, theme, and contents of each book.

In this connection it must be emphasized again that the student needs some understanding not only of Biblical history but also of the history and culture of the various nations which had contact with God's people in Old Testament times. Background books for this purpose are mentioned in Chapter 7. A knowledge of geography is also valuable to the student who desires to learn truths of God through His revelation of Himself in the Biblical history books of the Old Testament.

Interpreting Prophetic Passages

The interpretation of Old Testament prophetic passages is a most complex and difficult task. Only general guidelines and principles can be suggested here.

The purpose and function of the prophet are made clear in the Scriptures. He was called by God to be His spokesman. Prophets spoke words of warning and promise. Through dreams and visions and other ways God spoke to them of judgment and salvation, and they relayed God's message to the people. Their chief purpose was to admonish and encourage the people to faithfulness and godly living. Amos sounded the prophet's call when he cried out: "Prepare to meet your God, O Israel!" (Amos 4:12)

In carrying out their prophetic office, the prophets sometimes foretold future events, but they usually did this by speaking directly to the contemporary needs and problems of their hearers. In any case, their message was intended by God to create a response of penitence, love, and obedience. Prophecies of future events had the same purpose.

The proper interpretation of a prophetic passage, then, will be very practical and helpful. Sometimes people make the mistake of studying the prophets only to "learn" about future events. This approach, common to millennial groups, is likely to miss the divinely intended message and lesson. The possibility of getting the intended message will be increased if the following guidelines are kept in mind.

The Literal Meaning

Scriptural prophecy, we said in Chapter 3, can have only one intended meaning. This intended or single meaning is based upon careful study of the literal sense of the original words, although the intended or spiritual meaning may be something quite different from the literal meaning. The literal meaning is established by a careful study of the words and grammar *and* the historical situation of the prophet and his hearers or readers. The meaning of the historical and geographical allusions (see Hab. 1:6-11; Zeph. 2:8-9) and of the images and customs (see Micah 4:1-2;

Obad. 5) must also be correctly understood if they are to serve as a basis for a contemporary application.

Many interpreters pay little or no attention to the literal, original meaning. It is not surprising, therefore, that they can interpret passages to mean almost anything. During World War II, for example, supposedly competent Bible students were convinced that the number 666 (Rev. 13:11-18) referred to Adolf Hitler; others concluded that the reign of Josef Stalin was clearly foretold. In drawing the parallels, both groups had not done proper homework on the literal sense of the passage and had not stayed within the limits of the historical situation.

In some prophetic passages the literal sense of the words is the intended meaning. In Jer. 46:25-28, for example, Jacob and Israel are to be interpreted literally as the "then and there" people of God. (See also Jeremiah 36; Lamentations 1–5; Isaiah 27–28.) But then see Isaiah 60, where the literal meaning is not the intended meaning. The reasons are given in the following paragraphs.

The Figurative Meaning

A very sizable group of Bible students take the literal meaning of a prophetic passage to be the only meaning. They insist, for example, that a passage like Jer. 31:1-14 speaks of the actual restoration of the nation of Judah in the land of Palestine. The difficulty with this literal interpretation is that it then calls for the actual restoration of the physical nation of Israel and Judah and the actual reestablishment of full temple worship in the geographical city of Jerusalem.

In the New Testament, however, Jesus spoke against the restoration of temple worship (John 4:16-26), a point which was strongly underscored by the apostle Paul (Eph. 2:1-22). Furthermore, the New Testament clearly teaches that the new covenant (Jer. 31:31-34) was going to include people of all nations (1 Cor. 11:25; John 3:16-21; Eph. 2:11-22). So the prophet of God was evidently using the nation of Israel as a symbol of a spiritual Israel.

Thus the intended meaning of many prophetic passages is not the same as the literal or surface sense of the actual words. Difficulties arise in determining when the divinely intended meaning is the same as the literal sense and when a figurative or nonliteral meaning is intended. The long controversy about the 1,000-year reign of Christ on earth (Rev. 20:2) illustrates the problem perfectly. One group insists that this prophetic passage must be taken literally, while another group insists that the doctrine of the millennium is nowhere taught in a clear passage (*locus classicus*). Ps. 90:4 and 2 Peter 3:8 show that a "thousand years" is not always taken literally elsewhere in the Bible.

Most Roman Catholic and Protestant interpreters insist that the many Old Testament passages that speak of the restoration of the nation of Judah, the city of Jerusalem, and the temple are to be interpreted figuratively. They base their argument on the New Testament passages that speak of the Christian people as the new chosen people of God and the new temple. Other interpreters insist that these passages and New Testament passages like Rom. 11:25-32 are to be interpreted literally.

Is the reader frustrated by this dilemma? The reader must keep in mind, first, that much religious language is symbolic and dare not be interpreted literally and, second, that he has his own responsibility of deciding for a figurative or literal interpretation on the bais of the suggested principles. There may also be the need of withholding judgment on a particular passage until sufficient evidence warrants a judgment.

Prophecy and Fulfillment

Some Old Testament prophecies are specifically mentioned as having been fulfilled in the New Testament (Ps. 41:9 – John 13:18; Is. 7:14 – Matt. 1:22-23; Micah 5: 2 – Matt. 2:5-6; etc.). When this is the case, the student's search for the meaning of the prophecy is ended. But even in such cases, a useful distinction is made between direct and typological prophecies.

A direct prophecy is a statement that refers to nothing prior to New Testament times and that has its fulfillment solely in New Testament times. Micah 5:2 is an example of such a prophecy.

The prophecy about 30 pieces of silver, however, does not strike the reader as a prophecy at all when he first reads it in Zech. 11:1-14. The payment of 30 pieces was a transaction that took place in the life of Zechariah. In this case, Matthew (27:9-10), inspired by the Holy Spirit, enables the reader to see that in this event Zechariah was a type, that is, a predictive figure, of the Great Shepherd who would one day also be valued at 30 pieces of silver. Note how complete this typical or typological prophecy is, for the 30 pieces were even cast into the treasury, very much like the later action of Judas. In this case, there is no way of knowing how much Messianic meaning Zechariah's contemporaries saw in his strange action. Its "then and there" meaning, however, is clearly indicated in the context.

Likewise Is. 7:16 indicates that the famous prophecy of Is. 7:14 found a fulfillment in Isaiah's time before the great fulfillment recorded by St. Matthew. It is thus an "acted out" or typological prophecy. The New Testament enables the Bible student to appreciate the predictive, Messianic element of the incident. (See also Jer. 31:15 – Matt. 2:16-18 and Hos. 11:1 – Matt. 2:14-15.)

There are other Old Testament statements or actions which correspond in striking fashion to New Testament accounts but are not identified as fulfilled prophecies. In such cases, the student must make a careful comparison of the pertinent passages in both Testaments to determine if the common elements in the two are sufficient to indicate a relationship of promise and fulfillment. Paul and Peter refer to many examples of Old Testament types which foreshadow New Testament fulfillment (Gal. 4:21-31; 1 Cor. 5:6-8; Rom. 5:12-21; 1 Peter 2:9-10; 2:18-22). The Book of Hebrews is filled with typological interpretations of the Old Testament.

Apocalyptic Prophecy

In both Testaments there is a special kind of prophetic writing which has been identified only in rather recent years. It is called apocalyptic (ah-pock-uh-lip'-tik) writing. The word comes from a Greek word which means "revelation"; hence the last book in the New Testament is known either as the Revelation or the Apocalypse of St. John.

Apocalyptic passages are found in the Old Testament in the books of Isaiah (chs. 24—27), Joel, Zechariah (chs. 9—14), Daniel (chs. 7—12), and Ezekiel. In the New Testament most of the Revelation of St. John is apocalyptic in character (chs. 4—22). A glance at those sections reveals the dramatic use that apocalyptic writers made of images and symbols and also indicates that there are few references to identifiable historical places, events, and persons. In both these respects, apocalyptic prophecies differ from regular prophetic passages.

Apocalytic literature, like all other literary forms, was created to serve a particular need and a particular purpose. The student must understand this purpose if he is to do justice to its nature and meaning. Apocalyptic literature was created to assure God's people, in times when everything looked black to them, that God was in charge of history and would bring an end to the history of the world through a great cataclysm. He would thus deliver His chosen people from their oppressors and translate them into a perfect and never-ending world. God had set the time of destruction, and His victory was inevitable and assured.

Apocalyptic writers proclaimed this belief by employing strange symbols and visions and mysterious references to the passage of time prior to the end (Dan. 7:25; 9:24;

Rev. 20:1-10). It is believed by some scholars that apocalyptic writers employed strange symbols and time references so that the oppressing king or emperor would not learn that they were proclaiming his approaching defeat.

The keys to a right interpretation of apocalyptic literature are few and simple, but their correct use is very difficult. First, keep in mind the general purpose and theology of all apocalyptic literature as explained briefly above. This is basic and of first importance. Second, try to learn what the symbols and images meant to the first audience. A red horse symbolized war (Rev. 6:3); white usually symbolized innocence; a horn was a symbol of strength (Rev. 13:11; Dan. 8:1-14); water was, interestingly enough, often but not always a symbol of evil and destruction (Rev. 12: 13 – 13:4; but see also 22:1-2). Third, apocalyptic prophecies almost always require a figurative interpretation, unlike prophecy which may require a figurative or a literal interpretation. Fourth, avoid deriving any important religious idea solely or chiefly from apocalyptic passages (for example, the millennium). Unless an apocalyptic idea is taught elsewhere in a clear passage, we let the teaching which is found in apocalyptic passages occupy only a minor and perhaps even a questionable place in our system of Christian doctrine.

The Christological Principle

A basic principle for all Biblical study and therefore also for the interpretation of prophecy and apocalyptic passages is that Jesus Christ and the message of God's grace and love must be kept in the forefront at all times. 1 Peter 1:11 states this principle clearly: "They [the prophets] inquired what person or time was indicated by the Spirit of Christ within them when predicting the sufferings of Christ and the subsequent glory."

Clear New Testament statements about the person and work of Jesus Christ repeatedly open up the correct interpretation of Old Testament prophecies. He is the truth and the substance of all Old Testament types and shadows; He is the heart of the Old Testament, or covenant, of God's grace; He is the center and the meeting place of all God's promises. (See Luke 24:13-27.)

Interpreting Poetic Passages

Poetry is a very common literary form in the Old Testament. Approximately 150 chapters, plus the books of Psalms and Job (perhaps also Proverbs), are poetic in character. For the interpretation of Hebrew poetry there are several specific guidelines. It was not until the 17th and 18th centuries, by the way, that this particular literary form was identified. (Compare the typography of the Book of Isaiah in the King James and Revised Standard Versions.)

Poetry has its own forms and power and is particularly suited to the touching of people's emotions. It requires a sensitive, sympathetic, and responding heart on the part of the reader.

Some understanding of Hebrew poetry will be helpful to the Bible student. The first thing to remember is that its chief characteristic is a balance of thought and rhythm (called parallelism) rather than a balance of sound (rhyme) and rhythm. The parallel poetic structure frequently finds the second line repeating the thought of the first line. Ps. 144:3 is a good example. In this verse the Bible student sees that "son of man" is simply a repetition of "man"; it is not a veiled reference to the Son of Man. (See also Pss. 8:1-8; 147:1-4, 7-11; Prov. 23:24; Is. 32:1-5; etc.)

An examination of the Book of Proverbs reveals that the second half of many of its couplets states the opposite of the first half. This is also good Hebrew parallelism. There are five or six other parallel patterns employed by Hebrew poets. As a general rule, in poetry the figurative meaning is found more frequently than the literal meaning, but this does not excuse the student from attempting to learn the "then and there" meaning of the poetic passages.

Interpreting the Psalms

In interpreting the psalms, the Bible student first ought to try to identify the author and his situation as well as that of the first readers. In Chapter 4 this was called the important "then and there" meaning. Some of the psalms provide this information in subheads (see Pss. 90, 60, 63, 52, 54, 47, 51, etc.). Then the historical references within the psalm should be carefully studied. Many of the psalms, for example, are based on the great deliverance which God accomplished for His people in the Exodus (Pss. 74, 77, 78, 105, 106, etc.) and are songs of gratitude and thanksgiving for God's great acts of grace.

The correct study of *Messianic* psalms requires, in particular, the historical background. Psalm 16, which is generally recognized as a Messianic psalm, evidently was written by David to thank God for having delivered him from Sheol and the Pit. It is only Paul's use of v. 10 in Acts 13:35 which enables the Bible student to see a typological Messianic prophecy in this psalm. (See also, for example, Pss. 24, 47, 97, 98, 99.)

In studying Messianic psalms, the interpreter's best guide is the New Testament. It is a common error on the part of some sincere Bible students to decide that many psalms are Messianic (though they really are not) and then pay no further attention to the "then and there" meaning.

The so-called imprecatory psalms, which contain very harsh prayers for the destruction of the inspired writers' enemies (Pss. 109, 139, 140, 52, etc.), must be understood on their own terms. It is a mistake to judge them by the beautiful moral teachings of Isaiah, Micah, or even our Lord. Such psalms must be seen as coming from the heated and fervent heart of the psalmist who wants God to overthrow those who stand in God's way. Christians may not speak such harsh words, but they can be as distressed and disturbed when men try to oppose God.

Summary

This chapter discussed principles that are particularly helpful in the interpreting of the Old Testament. The central theme of the Old Testament was stressed heavily, namely God's intent and purpose to preserve for Himself a chosen people who would show forth His praises. We also discussed the importance of understanding the author's viewpoint in interpreting historical passages. After considering the nature and function of prophecy, we called attention to the principle that the single, divinely intended meaning may be either the literal or the figurative meaning. The interpretation of apocalyptic passages was given special mention. The chapter concluded with a summary of principles for interpreting Hebrew poetry.

TO HELP YOU REVIEW

1. Summarize in your own words the theme of the Old Testament. How does this insight help you relate the two Testaments to each other?

2. Explain the difference between literal and figurative meanings. Give an example of the misinterpretation of each.

3. What is a typical or typological event or passage in the Bible? Give an illustration of this kind of Messianic prophecy.

4. What is apocalyptic prophecy?

5. Give an example of how a knowledge of Hebrew poetry can help one to interpret passages from the Psalms.

6. Should Isaiah 52 be interpreted figuratively, or literally, or typologically? Why?

The study of New Testament writings will prove to be a comparatively easy undertaking for most Christians, since they are probably more familiar with them than they are with the Old Testament documents. But proper principles of interpretation are necessary, even though the subject matter is more familiar.

The Theme and Purpose of the New Testament

The first step is to gain a clear understanding of the basic theme of the New Testament. This is not quite as simple as it may sound, for there are several emphases in the basic theme. All the New Testament documents are centered in the person and work of Jesus Christ; they all acknowledge Him to be the Son of David and the Son of God, and they recognize Him as the world's Savior. Further, they all sound the note of victorious fulfillment and declare in one way or another that God has fulfilled all His promises and has perfected all His plans in Jesus Christ. This truth leads the New Testament writers to emphasize that the new age has dawned and that Jesus Christ has made all things new. (2 Cor. 5:17; Rev. 21:5)

The student of the Bible needs to understand and accept this announcement of victory and total newness if he is to do justice to any New Testament passage. Like the Old Testament, the New Testament also places considerable emphasis upon God's plan to create and preserve a chosen people, the new Israel, in Jesus Christ (1 Peter 2:9). And finally, the New Testament presents the Christian's joyful and willing life of worship and service. A sense of privilege and gratitude must seize those who study and accept these teachings of the New Testament.

New Testament History

Like the Old Testament, the New Testament is a book of history. This means several things for the study of the Bible. It means that the student must know something about the history of the New Testament world and its people. He needs to know the life of Jesus and the history of the New Testament church. Further, he must know something about the history of the Biblical world in the period between the Testaments. (400 B. C. – A. D. 1)

The New Testament reports that God came into the world's history as a human being in Jesus of Nazareth; that He was involved in the life, death, and resurrection of this Man who was crucified under Pontius Pilate; and that what happened in Galilee and Judea changed the future history of mankind completely. The Christian faith is not based on a system of thought or upon a writer's dreams and visions. It is based on historical happenings. This rootedness in history sets the Christian religion apart from other religions.

History of the Books

The limits of this text do not permit a full discussion of how the New Testament books were written, but a few words need to be said on this important topic. For approximately 20 years following Jesus' ascension, His followers had no books they could call uniquely their own. They shared the Old Testament books with the Jews. The first specifically Christian books were Paul's letter to the Galatians (written in A. D. 49, according to some scholars) and his two letters to the Thessalonians (A. D. 51). During this period sermons were preached about Jesus, and Christians told short stories about His life to each other and to non-Christians who would listen. An outline of the content of this preaching can be found in Acts 2:14-36; 3:11-26; 4:8-12; and 10:34-43.

The content of the preaching was quite simple. Peter's sermons were not delivered in the form of arguments or threats. He simply proclaimed the Gospel, the news of God's great deed in Jesus Christ. He functioned like a king's herald (Greek: *kerux* [kay'-ricks]) who announced that his master had gained a victory. Hence this announcement or proclamation is called the "kerygma" (kay'-rig-mah), and this type of preaching and teaching is "kerygmatic." During this period of oral communication of the Gospel, many stories about Jesus were being circulated by word of mouth or perhaps in brief written form. These stories confirmed and illustrated the apostolic kerygma.

The first written gospel was probably prepared between A. D. 60 and 65. The gospel writers apparently were inspired by God's Spirit to use these oral stories, which were circulated everywhere in the early church, as well as their own information and interpretations. Paul's letters, written between 49 and 62 or 63, seem to assume that his hearers were acquainted with the facts of Jesus' life, for he mentions practically no details (see 1 Cor. 11: 23-25, 15:1-7). He simply states the apostolic kerygma briefly and then explains what it means to be a follower of the risen Christ. John's Gospel (also his epistles and the Book of Revelation) were probably not written until after A. D. 90.

Some Bible scholars have indicated that the gospels (at least the first three gospels) consist of collections of short narratives about Jesus that circulated in the church in oral form for a number of years before they were written down by the evangelists. Many other stories may never have been written down (John 21:25). Each author selected those accounts and sayings that best suited his purpose. (Luke 1:1-4)

This insight into the origin and structure of the synoptic (first three) gospels was promoted by the school of Form Criticism which arose in Germany after World War I. The school has a bad reputation in the minds of many because some of its followers have argued that the life of Jesus in the synoptic books is not accurate or reliable and that the inspired authors were really unimaginative "scissors and paste" editors who put the short stories together in a mechanical and somewhat careless way to prove their own point of view concerning the person and work of Jesus.

In this book these radical conclusions are not accepted, but the theory of how the gospels came into being makes good sense. This theory (a point of view which has not been proved scientifically) explains many of the *similarities and differences* in the first three gospels and has proved to be helpful to Bible students.

Unity and Diversity

The gospel writers are in perfect agreement in their answer to the question about who Jesus is: "You are the Christ, God's promised Messiah." But each of the evangelists sees the Christ from a different point of view and presents a noticeably different picture of the meaning of His life and work. Each of the writers wrote from his own perspective, out of his own personal convictions, for a particular audience and purpose, and in his own unique style. The Bible student needs some understanding of the theme and purpose of each gospel in order to interpret it correctly and to get the greatest spiritual benefit from his study of the various accounts.

One example of a comparative study of the gospel accounts must suffice. The bulk of the first three gospels is very much alike, but the first two chapters of Matthew and Luke are completely different from each other, while Mark omits any reference to the birth and childhood of Jesus. The third chapter of Matthew and Luke correspond to Mark's first chapter.

What can be said about the authors' points of view from these differences? One thing is obvious: Mark decided that the Gospel account should begin with Jesus' public ministry, while Matthew and Luke felt that the birth and childhood of Jesus were important to their presentation of the Gospel. The reason why Matthew included the infancy narratives may be that there are four prophetic fulfillments in it; Matthew wanted to emphasize that Jesus is the promised Messiah. Luke, who is often called a historian as well as "the physician," used the infancy narrative perhaps to connect Jesus' birth with Roman history. (See Luke 2:1-2; also his historical note in 1:1-4.)

In the first two chapters Luke records four beautiful songs — perhaps because he was himself a poet, perhaps because he wanted to explain to Theophilus (Acts 1:1) the origin and full meaning of the hymns which the Christians were using in their worship. For this kind of comparative study of the gospels, a "gospel harmony" is very useful. In such a book, the four biographies of Jesus are printed in parallel columns so that the student can spot the similarities and differences at a glance.

The Quest for the Historical Jesus

Almost all contemporary interpretation of the four gospels works with a useful distinction between the

"Jesus of history" and the "Christ of faith." Although this distinction is often based on very technical study and often leads exegetes to conclusions which are unwarranted, something needs to be said about its good features and helpful contributions.

These labels are used by Bible students to express their belief that the four gospels were not intended to be diary-like, day-by-day biographies of the Jesus of history but were rather the kerygmatic confession of the writer and other early Christians. The term "the Christ of faith" is used by these Bible scholars to express their conviction that many of the statements about Jesus' life and work in the gospels are intended to show what the early Christians believed about Him. They are not to be thought of as accurate "photographs" of what He may actually have said or done.

For the past 200 years Bible students have asked themselves how much can be known about the actual life Jesus lived on earth. (This is what is meant by the phrase "Jesus of history.") Many feel it is necessary to find some way to determine what portions of the gospel accounts are historical fact and what stories were created by the faith of the first generation of Christians. This sorting out is necessary, they say, so that Christian faith can rest upon the *facts* of Jesus' life rather than upon the accounts gathered by later Christian writers.

Without going into this complex question in further detail, it is well to remember that the gospels also reflect the understanding and faith of the individual author and early Christian congregations. (Compare John 2:11 with Mark 8:14-21, for example.) And most important let the reader bear in mind that these books were given to the church by the inspiration of the Holy Spirit and are therefore completely reliable as a basis for faith to this very day.

The benefit of "the quest" lies in its emphasis that the gospels have come from the faith of the first generation of

Christians and that they are a call to Spirit-given faith in Jesus as the Christ, the Son of God and Savior of the world. "Confess Jesus to be the Christ, accept Him as the Savior, believe in His way of life, and follow Him completely, even as we did," say the gospels to the Bible reader of any time and place.

Interpreting the Parables

Jesus made extensive use of parables in His teaching; therefore a look at principles for their proper interpretation is in order. The parable was a very common literary form in Jesus' day and was widely used by rabbis. The parables teach by comparing a spiritual reality to a physical object or action. "The kingdom of the heavens is like a little bush which grows into a big tree," they would say; or, "The kingdom of heaven is like a man who sowed good seed in his field."

The following insights will be helpful. First, the parable does indeed teach by comparison; but in most, if not all, of Jesus' parables, there is only one point of comparison because the parable is intended to teach only a single truth. The single lesson of the parable of the Ten Virgins (Matt. 25:1-13), for example, is stated in v. 13: "Be constantly watchful." Even though the details may also have instructive symbolical meaning (for example, the midnight hour), the student must be doubly careful in the interpretation of details (for example, that 50 percent of all people will be saved). The medieval allegorists found many truths in the details of each parable but often failed to find the truth Jesus intended to teach.

Second, most of Jesus' parables are about the kingdom of God, as can be seen from the introductions. This indicates that the correct interpretation of the truth ought to say something about God's rule in men's hearts or about His matchless grace and patience or about the supreme

---

value of His kingdom or about the completely changed lives of those in whose hearts God rules or even about what happens to those who ignore or oppose God's kingdom. An interpretation which finds in the parable only a truth about proper moral living has missed the point. The parables put the spotlight on what God has done in Christ and on the radical newness of life in His kingdom—the life of His Spirit.

The Acts of the Apostles

The Acts of the Apostles yields its meaning rather quickly and easily. The book is an interesting account of the activities of Peter and Paul and some of their friends in the years between Christ's resurrection and Paul's first imprisonment in Rome, which occurred about A. D. 60 – 62. St. Luke, the author, states his theological point of view in Ch. 1:1-2 and 1:8:

"In the first book [the Gospel], O Theophilus, I have dealt with all that Jesus began both to do and teach, until the day when He was taken up, after He had given commandment through the Holy Spirit to the apostles whom He had chosen. . . . 'But you shall receive power when the Holy Spirit has come upon you; and you shall be My witnesses in Jerusalem and in all Judea and Samaria and to the end of the earth.' "

The book is to be read and studied as the inspired account of how the Holy Spirit empowered the apostles to carry on the work of heralding God's salvation to all people. This work was only begun by Jesus, said St. Luke. The Gospel was to be brought "to the end of the earth," a term used for the imperial capital of Rome in at least one contemporary non-Biblical document. In the judgment of some students of the book, Luke wanted to show Theophilus that God's actions moved in a straight line from His creation of a chosen people in the Old Testament, through the life and work of Jesus Christ, and into the time of every Christian reader of the Book of Acts.

There are several other principles which can make the study of the Book of Acts relatively easy and very interesting. First, the student must keep a good map of the New Testament world at hand so that he can familiarize himself with the locations of the places mentioned in the book. Second, he ought to study a good book on the archaeological discoveries and reconstructions in many of these places. Third, he ought to make a careful study of the points of contact between the Book of Acts and the epistles, especially those of St. Paul. Fourth, reading a history of this period of the church's life will prove helpful.

Furthermore, the reader must remember that many customs and situations in the life of the church have changed in 2,000 years and that he must distinguish carefully between the "then and there" meaning of a passage and the present-day applications of its meaning. However, this caution must not be overstressed, for in many Biblical passages the present-day meaning is the same as the original literal meaning (for example, Acts 2:14-28). But in other cases, the "then and there" meaning and the application must be carefully distinguished. For example, the literal meaning of 1:15-26 is that the early church selected Matthias to take the place of Judas so that the inner group of disciples would again total 12, a sacred and important number for the church. But this "then and there" meaning ought not to be made a law for any church body today. A modern application of this particular account would be that church leaders need to follow Jesus and live close to Him in order to serve Him. The "then and there" meaning of 2:44-45 is that the early Christians practiced a type of communal living and sharing. But times have changed so that this cannot be made a binding law on all church members today.

The epistles, or letters, make up a third of the New Testament. Their study becomes fairly easy and very rewarding if certain principles are kept in mind. The first thing to remember is that the New Testament letters are indeed letters. They are not carefully outlined books or painstakingly constructed gospels. They are rather informal communications written to meet very specific problems in the church.

It seems that at times the writers of the epistles did not go back over what they had written to make them read smoothly (see 2 Corinthians 1 – 10; Gal. 1:6-7; 1 Cor. 9:19-23; Rom. 8:12-17). The Letter to the Hebrews is an exception and, to a degree, so is Paul's Letter to the Romans.

The New Testament letters are very much like the ordinary Greek letters of that time, hundreds of which have been found in Egypt. First the writer identifies himself, which is a very sensible approach. Then follows a greeting in which the writer expresses the wish that peace and joy will come to the addressee. Then the writer describes his situation briefly, and this is followed by a paragraph which contains the heart of the letter. Usually the writer signed the letter himself even if he had dictated it to a public stenographer. The New Testament letters follow this same general outline. Like other letters of that period of history, the letters of the New Testament tend to be personal and warm and frequently provide precious insights into the writer's thoughts and feelings. (Gal. 2:11-14)

The study of the New Testament letters requires, second, a correct knowledge of why each one was written. This information can usually be pieced together from a study of the letter itself. Sometimes the Book of Acts also provides some information about the letters. For example, a study of 1 and 2 Corinthians (1 Corinthians 5 and 16; 2 Corinthians 1, 2, 10, and 13) and Acts 18 – 19 helps the reader to appreciate the strained relations which existed between Paul and many members of the Corinthian congregation. This study also enables the student to understand that the central issue in 2 Corinthians is the question of apostolic authority and its crucial role in the life of the church.

In the third place, the letters should be seen as gold mines of information on Christian doctrine and practice. The meaning of the Bible for one's daily life is often spelled out most fully and clearly here. This requires that the student have a good understanding of the analogy of faith to interpret correctly the doctrinal meanings of specific passages. For example, Phil. 2:12 appears to be an appeal to men to save themselves. A background understanding of the Christian faith and its central emphasis upon salvation as God's completed action in Jesus Christ and His undeserved gift of grace to man at once alerts the reader to the fact that his first interpretation of Phil. 2: 12 cannot be correct. Salvation is evidently used in a different sense here, so the reader's understanding of salvation by grace keeps him from a false interpretation of the passage.

Fourth, as was established previously, the student must begin with the "then and there" meaning of the passage. When Paul talks about the teachers in the church in Eph. 4:11, it is obvious that he did not have Christian day school teachers as such in mind. In most instances the passage can be *applied* to teachers in parochial schools, but this is not its literal meaning. The literal meaning of 1 Cor. 7:25-26 is that Paul discourages marriage "in view of the impending distress," by which the apostle may have meant the destruction of the world. The application ought not to be made to life-long vows of chastity, for these were not at all in Paul's mind (see vv. 27-28). A natural application would be that we ought to order and arrange our lives in such a way that we are always free and ready to greet our returning Lord.

In Chapter 4 reference was made to the importance of understanding key words and a suggestion was given for gaining this mastery. It is often quite important to the understanding of the epistles that the student be acquainted with word families. A word family includes the root word and all the related words.

The study of an entire word family often provides the clearest and fullest understanding of what a word means in a specific passage. This study is carried on most satisfactorily with the Greek and Hebrew word families, but the study of English families can also be quite helpful.

One very large Biblical word family centers on the parent word "just." It includes such words as judge, judgment, justice, justify, justification, justly, and justifier. All of these words have somewhat different meanings, but a study of Biblical usage and the use of a good English dictionary uncovers their basic meaning, namely the idea of being fully and exactly right with the law. This is the description of a just man. The judge must decide if a person has acted justly. The lawyer attempts to justify his client's conduct.

Such a study of the word family casts a bright light on the meaning of members of this family in each passage where they occur. For example, in Biblical usage the word "just" carries the meaning of a strict law or standard according to which things are judged (1 Cor. 2:15; 4: 4). In Rom. 3:20-24 it has this meaning plus the further meaning that God, the just Judge, justifies man in an absolutely unique way. He declares the people just who accept Jesus Christ as their Savior.

Thus the word in this Romans passage begins with the important basic meaning of the word family but then adds to it a special Biblical meaning which is all-important to Christians. Other important word families center in such words as righteousness, love, knowledge, humility, faith, glory, goodness, and so forth.

The Letter to the Hebrews is of special interest to the Bible student. It is unfortunate that many Christians make little or no use of it because they do not understand how to interpret it. A few guidelines may help to unlock its message.

In all likelihood the letter was written to a group of Jewish Christians who were discouraged because they had lost many of their Jewish friends and had suffered some persecution for their faith. The writer of this letter wanted to point out to them the wonderful newness of life which Jesus Christ had brought so that they would resist the pressure to fall back into their former Old Testament religion.

To make this newness clear, the author culls from the Old Testament many prophetic types of Jesus so that his readers would understand that the Old Testament religion was incomplete and imperfect when compared to the New. The inspiring Spirit of God led the writer to find Old Testament prophetic types, or typological prophecies, of Jesus in such institutions and persons as Moses, the sabbath, the high priest, Melchizedek, the tabernacle, the old covenant, and the Law. In a very effective way the writer alternates between a discussion of an Old Testament type and down-to-earth admonition and encouragement. (See 1:14 and 2:1-4; 2:5-18 and 3:1; 3:2-19 and 4:1-2; and so forth. Note the important "therefores!")

The Revelation of St. John

The guidelines for interpreting Old Testament apocalyptic literature fit this New Testament book also.

Summary

To interpret the New Testament correctly, it is necessary to understand its basic theme of final victory and radical newness made available by God through His Son Jesus Christ. This theme is sounded clearly and with certainty in the kerygma of the apostles, who concentrated on the proclamation of who Jesus was and what He had done. It was not until 30 years after Christ's death and resurrection that kerygmatic stories about Him began to be written down in the form of gospels. The Holy Spirit led each gospel writer to present his own portrait of the meaning of Jesus' person and work. Because of this it is helpful to study the gospels comparatively with the use of a "harmony." Such studies help one to understand the distinct message of each book.

The Acts of the Apostles presents the continuation of God's Old Testament activity in the work of Jesus Christ and in the deeds of the apostles Peter and Paul and the first generation of Christians. The epistles are best studied as warm and informal letters written without careful polish to meet pressing practical problems in the first Christian congregations to which they were addressed. The student must understand why the epistles were written and must frequently differentiate between the "then and there" meaning and the present-day application of that meaning. The Letter to the Hebrews is a vivid demonstration of the way in which many incomplete typological prophecies of the Old Testament were fulfilled in Jesus Christ, who thus introduced a magnificent New Testament or covenant between God and His people.

TO HELP YOU REVIEW

1. How would you summarize the basic theme of the New Testament in your own words?

2. What is meant by the statement: "The New Testament is a history book"?

3. Characterize and summarize the apostolic preaching or *kerygma* on the basis of Peter's four sermons in the opening chapters of the Book of Acts. What is the relationship of the four gospels to this apostolic message?

4. Explain the place of oral tradition in the formation of the gospels.

5. What is Form Criticism? Why does it have a bad name in the minds of many? How can at least one of its principles help in the interpretation of the gospels?

6. What is meant by "the quest for the historical Jesus"? Can it contribute anything to our interpretation of the gospels?

7. What principles must be kept in mind when one interprets parables? What mistake did the allegorists make in the interpretation of the parables?

8. What was the nature and pattern of letters in the days of St. Paul? How does this knowledge help you to interpret New Testament epistles?

9. What is the chief key to the proper understanding of the Letter to the Hebrews?

This chapter consists of a laboratory demonstration of Biblical interpretation. The hermeneutical principles that were discussed in the first six chapters will be put to work in this one. The text is Mark 9:2-10. We shall follow a step-by-step method which is much the same as that used by professional exegetes. The reader need not expect to find as much in an ordinary study of a passage as this chapter will demonstrate is possible, but practice will soon enable most persons to follow these steps with considerable ease and spiritual benefit.

Helpful books as well as techniques will be discussed briefly in this chapter. Old Testament books and tools will also be mentioned, although they have little connection with the interpretation of this New Testament text. The most useful tools will be marked with one or more asterisks whenever this grading system seems appropriate. Three asterisks indicate books that should prove helpful to every Bible student. Two asterisks point out books that require more time and effort to reap their benefits. One asterisk indicates books that will help the exceptional lay Bible student, even though they are chiefly intended for the professional exegete. Undoubtedly none of the items mentioned will be completely acceptable or satisfactory to any one reader.

Step 1: Genuine and Continual Prayer

It is of great importance that the student form the habit of beginning his studies of a Biblical text with prayer and of continuing in a spirit of prayer. This is good exegetical practice, because only as the Spirit of God directs the Bible student and opens his eyes will he be led into truth and see wondrous things. Failure to employ prayer for the gift of God's Spirit can nullify the best hermeneutical principles.

Step 2: Establishing the Text

The passage we have chosen for basic study in this chapter is Mark 9:2-10. A study of selected English versions shows that there are no major variations among the ancient manuscripts. The RSV (Revised Standard Version) and the NEB (New English Bible) do not have in their footnotes the comments "Other ancient authorities add" or "Some witnesses read." (See Mark 9:29, 38 in the RSV for examples of important variations. Note that the NEB editors disagree with the RSV editors and in v. 38 place the phrase "who does not follow us" into the accepted text. Where this kind of disagreement exists among scholars, the reader of this book is advised to follow, as a general rule, the text he prefers.)

A footnote introduced by the word "Or" in either the RSV or the NEB indicates that a choice of translations is permitted by the Greek text. These footnotes are often very helpful in casting further light on the meaning of a word or phrase. Thus in Mark 9:7 there is a Greek word which can be translated rightly by either "only" or "beloved," even though the Greek word in the strictest sense means "only begotten."

Step 3: Grammar Analysis

Chapter 4 discussed the importance of knowing basic

rules of grammar. It was also pointed out that as a general rule the student of the English Bible does not encounter vexing grammatical problems that he must solve. This is true of the passage under study. There are several grammatical features, however, which cast helpful light on the final interpretation. The grammatical construction of v. 3 reveals the difficulty which Peter (or James or John) experienced when he tried to put his overpowering experience into words which others could understand. Note also the change from the singular subject in the first half of v. 6 to the plural subject in the second half; Peter is evidently the impetuous spokesman for the frightened men.

Step 4: Using Historical Information

Very early in his study of a passage, the student must answer the basic historical questions about the book itself. For this passage in Mark he might turn to the fine introduction to the New Testament by Martin H. Franzmann (*The Word of the Lord Grows***). This book provides the following answers to questions of authorship, date, and so forth.

Who: Mark, the son of Mary, the fear-filled companion of Paul, dear friend of Peter (the young man in the garden? Mark 14:51-52).

Where: Rome.

When: The 60s of the 1st century.

Why: To answer the questions of "converts who, once they had heard the basic *kerygma,* naturally and rightly asked, 'How did this great Good News that has revolutionized our lives begin? What is its history? Tell us more of the strong Son of God who loved us and gave Himself for us. Recount for us His words and work, which will make clear His will for us who have become His own.'"

To whom: Roman Christians (perhaps mostly

Gentiles) at the time of Nero, a Roman emperor who persecuted the Christians after the city of Rome had been devastated by fire.

(A good introduction to the books of the Old Testament is Edwin Redlich, *An Introduction to Old Testament Study for Teachers and Students*.)

The second kind of historical question calls for the interpreter to look at his geography and history books as he seeks to gain more background information for the understanding of a specific text. The geographic location of the incident in Mark appears to be a high mountain near the villages of Caesarea Philippi (Mark 8:27). The atlas shows Caesarea Philippi about 25 miles northeast of the Sea of Galilee, about the same distance inland from the Mediterranean Sea, and about 12 miles south of magnificent snow-covered Mount Hermon (was this the peak?), visible 40 miles or more to the south. So it is noteworthy that the inspiring and faith-strengthening transfiguration should take place outside of Palestine on a deserted mountain peak.

Additional information about the place can be gathered from a good Bible atlas such as the *Westminster Historical Atlas to the Bible**** and *Baker's Bible Atlas*** edited by Charles F. Pfeiffer. Books on Biblical archaeology provide valuable cultural and religious information. Two good works are John Thompson, *Archaeology and the Bible,* and Merrill Unger, *Archaeology and the New Testament.*

Is there anything in the history or culture of New Testament times that would cast light on our chosen text? It is necessary that the student read a standard history of this period for general background information. (Recommended are Merrill C. Tenney, *New Testament Times,*** and William F. Arndt, *New Testament History: A Survey of the Life of Christ and the History of the Apostolic Church,* rev. ed.***) From a good history book the interpreter would learn that the Jewish people expected

Elijah to reappear to introduce the messianic age. He would learn something about the kind of messiah for whom many Jews were waiting—an earthly, political deliverer. This would help him to understand why Jesus was not acceptable to them. It also suggests why the revelation of His true glory in the transfiguration was so important to the three disciples for they, too, had confused ideas about Jesus' messiahship.

The student would also profit by reading a history of the period from Malachi to our Lord's birth, for in these centuries most of the beliefs and attitudes of Jesus' countrymen were developed. (Carl G. Howie's *The Creative Era**** is helpful, as are chapters 1—5 of Tenney's book. Good books on the history of Old Testament Israel are John Bright's *The History of Israel*** and Gleason L. Archer's *Survey of the Old Testament*.** Good at a more popular level is Arthur W. Klinck's *Home Life in Bible Times: A Study in Biblical Antiquities*.)

A final important historical question remains: What did this passage mean to the first readers? What was its "then and there" meaning? It is best to delay answering this question until further information has been considered.

Step 5: Determining the Literary Form

This manual has repeatedly stressed the importance of determining the literary form in which a passage is cast. Failure to perform this step carefully and correctly can cause considerable confusion in determining the divinely intended meaning. The Mark passage is best classified as a historical narrative in form. It sets out to report an experience which Peter, James, and John had on a mountain. So the interpreter may rightly take the words in their normal and simplest meaning. There is nothing in the literary form itself which suggests that any of the words are used poetically, symbolically, parabolically, or in any other special literary way.

This step calls for the student to mark those words that appear to him to be noteworthy in the passage under study. In this case he would perhaps underline "transfigured," "Elijah," "Moses," "tabernacles" (KJV) or "booths" (RSV), "cloud," and "voice." Such a selection would provide rich interpretative material.

Word studies can be carried out in many ways. We might, for example, study the cross-references, for one or more of them may cast light on parallel word meanings. Bibles will vary in the cross-references they provide. One KJV edition suggests Dan. 7:9, which provides no information on the meaning of any of the key words but does suggest for later study the phrase "white as snow." Matt. 28:3 provides further light on Mark 9:3, and the two references suggest that this verse may be important for determining the final meaning of the Mark account. The cross-references in the RSV provide little help for our study of word meanings. They do call the reader's attention to other places in the New Testament that report a heavenly voice. This is very useful information for a later step. People who know Greek can find the best group of cross-references in the *Greek New Testament* * by Erwin Nestle and Kurt Aland.

A second very rewarding method of word study requires the use of a concordance. In this step the student turns to a key word and notes other passages where it is used in the Scriptures. The word "tabernacle," for example, has several interesting meanings in the Scriptures. It can mean an ordinary dwelling place or temporary shelter, the portable wilderness church, or, in symbolic language, the place where God dwells. The student learns to make notes of his findings, for at the early stages of his study he cannot know which pieces of information will be helpful to him in determining his final interpretation of a text.

As a general rule the concordances printed in Bibles,

even good study Bibles, are not adequate for word-study purposes. Alexander Cruden's *Popular Concordance*** (first published, by the way, in London in 1737) is widely used by Bible students. The "exhaustive" concordances edited by James Strong** or Robert Young** are very valuable tools for the interpreter's library. Thomas Nelson publishes a concordance** of the RSV text for those who prefer to work with this version. *The Oxford Concise Concordance*** is a short but quite helpful concordance of the RSV.

So-called topical Bibles are a different type of concordance that often prove to be very helpful. In the topical Bible the editor groups under a variety of topics those Bible passages which he feels provide basic insights into the topic. A well-known topical Bible is the *Thompson Chain Reference Bible*,** which is excellent. *The Harper Topical Concordance**** and *Nave's Topical Bible**** are easier to use, although their list of topics is shorter.

The student might have looked up the key words in a theological wordbook or in a good Bible dictionary. The wordbooks edited by Alan Richardson (*A Theological Word Book of the Bible***) and Jean-Jacques von Allmen (*A Companion to the Bible***) provide rich diets of theological insights concerning the meaning of many key words. The reader must keep in mind that these are *theological* wordbooks; that is, they represent the authors' understanding of the theology and the teaching of the Bible. Therefore they ought not to be used uncritically but need to be "tried" in the light of one's own study of the Biblical text.

A good Bible dictionary can serve some of the purposes of a theological wordbook. *The Westminster Dictionary of the Bible**** or *Unger's Bible Dictionary,**** for example, provides the student with a wealth of background information on booths or tabernacles. The dictionary articles remind the reader that booths played an important role in the celebration of one of the three great

Israelite feasts. This item may suggest to the student something of what may have been in Peter's mind when he made his seemingly strange suggestion. *The Concordia Bible Dictionary**** is a more concise reference work.

Step 7: Studying the Text in Context

Chapter 4 called the reader's attention to the four circles of context in which every text must be studied. The first circle is that of the immediately preceding and following verses. Mark 8:27 begins the immediate context of our passage under study. Jesus withdrew from Galilee to Caesarea Philippi with His disciples. He asked them what they thought of Him, and Peter responded with the confession that Jesus was God's promised Messiah.

This great confession was followed by our Lord's first clear prediction of His suffering, death, and resurrection. It was truly a moment of truth and a time of testing for the puzzled disciples (8:32-33). Then Jesus presented His blunt demands of discipleship in unmistakable terms. This is followed by the transfiguration account.

Then our Lord commanded the three disciples (9:9) to tell no one about their experience until the Son of Man should have risen from the dead. The immediate context concludes with the story of the epileptic lad whom the nine disciples could not heal. The entire context is one of challenge and decision, a challenge to accept Jesus as God's Christ because they had seen His glory and a decision to follow Him in the path of suffering and service even to the least of God's children.

The second context is that of the book itself. The best way to determine the meaning of this context is to read and study the book for yourself. Further help can be gotten from almost any introduction to the New Testament or any commentary on Mark's Gospel (see below, Step 9), for these books usually provide outlines of the thought development of the books which they discuss.

St. Mark's Gospel presents a striking picture of Jesus as the powerful Son of God. But His divine power was not recognized or confessed by the great majority of those who knew Him or heard Him. Only those whose eyes had been opened by the Spirit hailed Him as God's Messiah (4: 10-12). The gospel vividly describes how this Spirit-given understanding rose above the disciples' natural and persistent confusion, ignorance, blindness, and fear; how they clung to Jesus despite the fact that almost everyone else had rejected Him; how they were still perplexed at the moment of His resurrection (16:8); and how they were finally so convinced by the Spirit that Jesus was the Christ that they preached this good news everywhere (16: 20). This portrait of Jesus' Messiahship and of the very human disciples must have been a source of great comfort and inspiration to the Roman Christians, who very likely were being persecuted by Nero for their faith. Perhaps the Spirit inspired Mark to paint the picture in just this way because the Roman Christians needed this sermonic gospel then and there.

The third circle of context calls for the study of the other works of the writer. In the case before us this step can be passed over, for the gospel is the only Biblical book written by St. Mark. In the case of the writings of Paul, John, and Peter, this third step often can be quite helpful.

The fourth circle is that of the entire Bible. To make this step meaningful, the student needs a fairly good understanding of the major themes and motifs of the Bible. General observations, however pious they may be (to the effect, for example, that the Bible records God's plans for man's salvation), are of little help here.

Three themes from the context of the entire Bible provide help for interpreting the text. The one theme of overarching significance is that of God's repeated promise to come into man's life and deliver him. The heavenly voice in our passage points to the greatest and final fulfillment of this theme. The three disciples are privileged to hear this great announcement!

The second specific theme of considerable importance for interpreting the Mark passage centers in the Biblical concept of God's glory. In the Old Testament it was reflected from the face of Moses after he had been on the mountain which was covered by a cloud and the glory of the Lord (Ex. 24:12-18; 34:1-35). The glory of the Lord also filled the tabernacle (Ex. 40:34-38) and the temple (1 Kings 8:1-11). In Mark the glory of the Lord appears in the transfigured Jesus and perhaps also in the cloud.

The third theme from the context of the entire Bible centers in the idea of God dwelling or "tabernacling" with man. In the Old Testament His dwelling was centered in the tabernacle or the temple. In the New Testament it centers in Jesus Christ, and therefore locally built booths or tabernacles are no longer needed. Where two or three are gathered in the name of Jesus, God will dwell in their midst! Other themes could also be applied to this event, but these three will illustrate how specific themes from the context of the entire Bible help to illuminate a given passage.

This understanding of the context of the entire Bible comes through much reading and study of the Scriptures. But there are some tools which will help the interpreter gain this kind of mastery. The theological wordbooks mentioned above will often prove helpful in this respect. Good commentaries will usually be helpful, too.

Of special value are books on Biblical theology. These books have become very popular in the last 15 years and are designed by the authors to analyze one or more of the basic theological themes of the Bible. One of the earliest and best is John Bright's *The Kingdom of God*.** As the title suggests, Bright believes that the idea of God's kingdom or reign is the central theological theme of the Bible.

A special kind of contextual study which is helpful for the interpretation of passages from the synoptic gospels is the comparison of the parallel accounts in one or two of the other synoptic gospels. Here the careful study of the *similarities* and the *differences* in each account can provide valuable insights concerning the theological purpose of each writer. *A Synopsis of the Gospels* by H. F. D. Sparks is useful for this kind of study.

Step 8: Checking Other Translations

At this stage it will prove quite helpful to consult several other translations. In this way the student and interpreter may obtain other insights on word meanings or on the meaning of the entire passage. This step will also prove quite valuable in suggesting ways in which the interpreter's insights can be communicated to his audience. Helpful English versions are the *Revised Standard Version,* the *New English Bible, The New Testament in Modern English, The New Testament in the Language of Today* by W. F. Beck, *The New Testament in Modern English* and *Four Prophets* by J. B. Phillips, *A New Translation of the New Testament* by James Moffat, *The New Testament in Modern Speech* by R. F. Weymouth, and *The Bible: An American Translation* by E. J. Goodspeed.

At this point many interpreters find it helpful to write out the text in their own words and to incorporate into their version some of the insights which they have gained.

Step 9: Consulting the Commentaries

The discussion of commentaries has been deliberately postponed to this point. They should never be the first resort. They are, of course, valuable tools when they are used correctly, but they can interfere with the development of one's own interpretive skills.

Each commentary has its strong points and its weak points, and as the interpreter becomes familiar with various books he will find himself using them for different purposes.

Their basic role in the task of Biblical intepretation is to provide the student with a convenient, readily accessible way of testing his own findings. If he finds that the conclusions he has reached in going through the first eight steps lead him to quite different conclusions than those of the commentator, he needs to check his work carefully once more. Having done this, he may decide that he is still right and the commentator is wrong. Then it is up to the student to "argue" with the commentator and show that his interpretation is more in harmony with good principles of interpretation than that of the writer. In such a process the student will grow greatly in Biblical mastery.

Commentaries often provide additional cross-references and historical and cultural background which serve to illuminate a Biblical text. Or they may present theological and doctrinal insights which the student finds stimulating and helpful.

In some respects it is better to buy specific commentaries for individual books rather than a series for the entire Bible. It is encouraging to note that each year sees the appearance of additional commentaries in paperback for laymen.

Some lay interpreters (teachers) like to have a one-volume commentary on the entire Bible on their shelves so they can find help on almost any passage when they need it. Among the better one-volume commentaries are *A New Commentary on the Holy Scriptures, Including the Apocrypha*** edited by Charles Gore, Henry Goudge, and Alfred Guillaume; *A Commentary on the Bible*** edited by Arthur S. Peake and Alexander J. Grieve; and *The New Bible Commentary,* edited by F. Davidson, A. M. Stibbs, and E. F. Kevan.

The Layman's Bible Commentary*** is a series commentary, most of which is good. The same can be said of the *Cambridge Bible for Schools and Colleges.**** Two other series for laymen now in the process of appearing are the *Tyndale New Testament Commentaries*** and the *Wycliffe Bible Commentary*.**

Step 10: The "Then and There" Meaning

The student is ready now to take the crucial second-last step, that of establishing the "then and there" meaning of the text. By now the various facets of this meaning should be clear to the interpreter. The first readers undoubtedly saw in this text the meaning that Jesus was hailed by a voice from heaven as the Father's beloved or only Son, that He was transfigured and for a moment revealed something of His heavenly glory, that the appearance of Elijah and Moses emphasized our Lord's connections with the Old Testament, that for some reason this revelation took place in a deserted place and was witnessed by only three disciples, and that the entire incident revealed God's wonderful presence in man's world through Jesus and the way in which He would tabernacle among men.

It was also suggested that Mark's account may have said to the first readers that Jesus Christ often conceals or reveals His glory and His power in ways that puzzle His followers. Thus they may have found in this passage an inspiring challenge to continue to believe even though at times it may have seemed that their Master did not possess or use His divine power and glory in their behalf.

Step 11: The "Here and Now" Meaning

In the case of our text under study, the "here and now" meaning is almost identical with the "then and there" meaning described in Step 10. Modern Christians need to learn each of the lessons mentioned in the preceding section, and their faith will be enriched and strengthened in the measure that they do. Every interpreter can find a variety of applications of this divinely intended meaning.

Step 12: Living the Word

The preceding 11 steps have been designed to bring the student to this final step, which calls for him to "translate" the Word of God from the pages of the Book into his daily life and living. To take this step without taking the first 11 steps is to run the grave risk of finding in the Bible only those truths or lessons which the student wants to find. The discipline of proper hermeneutics enables the student to hear with growing accuracy and faithfulness what *God* is saying to him in a passage. Even then the truths which the student finds are usually shaped and influenced by the special needs or problems he is facing.

In this book we have distinguished between the *interpretation* of a passage, that is, the uncovering and defining of its divinely intended meaning, and the *application* of a passage, that is, the translating of the meaning and truth into present-day terms. Furthermore we have stressed that the interpretation of a passage can yield only one meaning, while the applications based on a passage may be many.

Step 12 begins with a review of the interpretation, that is, the lesson which God intends to teach. In the transfiguration passage, for example, our study helped us to see the meaning of the incident in (1) the fulfillment of God's old covenant promises in Jesus Christ; (2) the divine glory which God's Son possessed; (3) the close connection between the Testaments, as evidenced by the appearance of Moses and Elijah; and (4) the confusion which gripped the disciples as they tried to understand what was happening.

Working with these truths the Bible student and the

Sunday school teacher can draw several basic applications to his living and to his teaching: (1) the student is prompted to confess that Jesus is the promised Messiah and is led to worship Him; (2) the student is assured of the fulfillment of God's plan of salvation. These applications flow quite naturally from the interpretation.

Several more applications suggest themselves to most students of this passage even though they are, perhaps, not as directly related to what the passage says. On the basis of the phrase in v. 8, "but Jesus only," some determine to live more completely for Jesus. Students of this passage also are encouraged to serve Jesus and their fellowmen as they note that the disciples were not permitted to remain on the mountain. They had to go down into the valley and face the problems of their fellowmen. These suggested applications do not exhaust the possibilities in this text.

Schoolchildren will find other applications in this text, for their needs and understandings are different. The same is true for other age groups. This great richness in application is part of the gift of the Spirit God has given us in His Word. While the Word of God in the Bible does not change in meaning, it remains up-to-date through the art of lively application, the highest art of the Sunday school teacher.

TO HELP YOU REVIEW

1. What is the importance of knowing who wrote a Biblical book and why, where, and when it was written? How can such information be obtained by the beginning Bible student?

2. Does Dan. 7:9-14 provide helpful insights for interpreting the transfiguration account? If so, how?

3. Why is a concordance an essential tool of the Bible student?

4. What signs in a text suggest where the immediate context begins and ends?

5. How should commentaries be used?

6. What guidance would you give to a fellow Christian who asks your opinion about what modern versions he should use?

A famous thinker once described good education as that which happens when a teacher sits on one end of a log and the pupil on the other. This observation reminds the teacher that good education depends in large measure on teacher-pupil relations and on what the teacher is as a person.

One of the most common failings of Sunday school teachers is an inadequate mastery of the subject they teach. The blind cannot lead [or teach] the blind, said Jesus. Teachers must grasp and possess God's Word of truth and light and life before they can truly communicate it to others. This chapter suggests ways whereby the material in this book can contribute to better teaching of the Bible.

Biblical Interpretation and Personal Growth

A Privilege and a Necessity

Our knowledge of God is never perfect in the present life, and our use of God's power is always very limited. As a consequence Christians are sometimes as puzzled about life's meaning as are non-Christians. They are also distressed at times by life's problems and troubles. But Christians who want to grow in knowledge and power are reminded again that the basic element in a program of spiritual growth is Bible study.

It has frequently been observed that Christians can never stand still with respect to their faith. It is either increasing or decreasing. Increase calls for regular, prayerful, serious study of God's Word and the living of it. But the Christian also knows that God has promised His Holy Spirit to help those who "tremble at His Word." Time and effort devoted to Bible study offer great spiritual dividends to the church school teacher. But the teacher must decide to put forth the effort to grow in the knowledge and right understanding of the Bible.

Reading or Interpreting?

In the past, Bible study for many Christians consisted mainly in the reading of a text and a rather disorganized surface commentary on isolated verses by the leader. While some improvement in Bible study methods has been observed in recent years, almost every church education leader admits that modern Christians, too, make very unsatisfactory use of their Bibles.

This book is aimed at helping Christians to become students and *interpreters* of the Bible rather than mere readers and listeners. There are at least two important differences between interpreters and passive listeners. Interpreters try to discover for themselves what God is saying and good interpreters observe and follow good principles of interpretation. Second, interpreters who are students and teachers are almost forced to live more closely and more constantly with their Bibles than Christians who settle for secondhand knowledge, and this gives them a greater measure of spiritual power. The kind of study of the Bible outlined in this book is a direct inducement to regular personal use of the Bible.

Profitable Bible use depends upon the gift of the Holy Spirit. This point has been stressed several times already. It is only the Holy Spirit who understands the deep things of God (1 Cor. 2:6-13), and it is He who must communicate these deep things of spiritual truth to us.

Fortunately our Savior has promised that he who truly asks and seeks and knocks shall receive and find God's Spirit. It is this openness to the voice and the guidance of the Holy Spirit that makes proper usage of the Bible so rewarding. As a Christian studies the Bible prayerfully and thoughtfully, he is engaged in conversation and communion with the Spirit of God and of Christ. In such "dialog" with God, the Spirit opens eyes of faith to wonderful truths of salvation and guides the student in the way he should go.

Three Basic Steps

Most Biblical interpreters agree that Spirit-directed Bible study and teaching involve three basic activities or stages: investigation, reflection, and application.

Investigation

Investigation calls for careful study of a passage. For this the methods described in Chapters 3 to 7 will prove helpful, even if not always necessary in every detail. The goal of this first stage is to discover what the text really says. For example, the words of Is. 50:1 say that God has divorced Israel's mother and has sold His children to pay His debts. The reader of these words realizes immediately that the sentence as it reads cannot be the divinely intended meaning, but in any case, the student rolls up his sleeves and first gets at the meaning of words and terms, a study of the context, of the historical background, and so forth.

Reflection

In this next stage the student must try to answer the question: What is the meaning of the passage? Considerable space was devoted to the study of how one learns to recognize the divinely intended *meaning* of the words of Holy Scripture. This meaning, truth, revelation of God, and principle of life — the Gospel — is more than sounds of syllables and words and usually more than the sum of words and their *apparent* meaning.

To determine the meaning of a word or passage such as Is. 50:1, meditation is required, particularly critical thinking and *reflection*. To "get" the intended meaning, the general purpose and message of God's Word, a review of the purpose of the Book of Isaiah and a further study of the context, both literary and historical, must be considered — and all this in a sincere desire to know the *truth*.

Such Spirit-guided study will lead the student of Is. 50:1 to understand that the references to divorce and slavery are figurative. They are a very effective means of conveying the message that the people of God were in their wretched situation because Mother Israel had been unfaithful to God and had thereby sold her children into slavery. The Lord, their heavenly Father, had not willed the divorce. The passage obviously does not mean that God approves of divorce or slavery in the human, physical sense of the terms.

Application

The third task calls for the teacher and student to ask: What does this passage say to me and to others living in *today's* world? This, too, requires meditation or reflection, but of a different kind, and also calls for action — obedience (doing) and experience (living).

What is God saying to me? How should I apply it to my life? What is it saying about life today? What commitment and response is it calling for on the part of the church, of which I am a part, as well as the world?

In the sense of application, one may speak of many "meanings" of a passage, and the expresson is often used in this broad sense. Strictly speaking, however, there is only one divinely intended general or generic meaning in each passage. The Bible student needs to keep this distinction in mind to avoid confusion concerning what God is saying in the Bible.

The student might make several different applications of Is. 50:1. The passage could move him to sorrow at the thought of his own frequent rebellion against God. The marriage picture might remind him of God's love and faithfulness toward His wife and children in the new covenant and therefore to him and all believers in Christ. It may inspire him to greater love for the covenant God, to an increased struggle against sin in his own life, and to more faithful obedience and active service to this God of Israel, who is also *his* God. All of these applications or "meanings" flow from careful and proper investigation and meditation. They are not forced upon the text or drawn arbitrarily to suit the fancy of the interpreter.

The Psychology of Personal Meanings

But the line from interpretation (What does the text mean?) to application (What does it mean to me?) is not always as direct as it was described in the preceding paragraph. The line always passes through the mind and heart of the student, and the effect of these factors is often unpredictable. Several other elements play into the picture and affect the *personal* meaning or application which each student may find in a passage. These elements may even affect the interpretation, or the divinely intended meaning, which the student draws from the text.

There is, first, the matter of preconceived opinions, presuppositions, and prejudices, which everyone has and which are often very hard to identify and put aside. For example, many people have the preconceived conviction that the responsibility for working out their own life flows from the dignity and freedom of man as a human being. This opinion prevents a right interpretation (and thus also a right application) of passages which speak of salvation as God's gracious gift in Jesus Christ. Frequently people with such a false assumption define grace to mean special spiritual help that God gives to the person who is working hard to save himself.

Presuppositions and Hermeneutical Systems

Philosophical presuppositions held by the interpreter also deserve a word in this connection. The dictionary defines a presupposition as "an antecedent logical condition." For example, conversation between two people is based on the presupposition, the required antecedent logical condition, that they both understand the words they use in approximately the same way.

This book on interpreting the Bible is based on several key presuppositions. These "antecedent logical conditions" are the belief that God is a personal God who has communicated His life-giving Word to man, that the Bible is inspired and inerrant and therefore free from contradictions, that God created and preserves the world, that miracles can happen, and so forth. Not all of these are "logical" in one sense of the word, but they are antecedent conditions which decisively affect Scriptural interpretations.

Much of the confusion in Christendom today is really caused by the failure to recognize how a man's presuppositions may affect his interpretation at least as much as the methods he uses. Many interpreters assume that the Bible is only the human record of the religious struggles of the

Hebrew people; or they do not believe that miracles can happen (the closed universe idea), including the Incarnation and the Resurrection. Obviously the interpretative conclusions of the latter group will differ from the conclusions reached by those who accept the presuppositions of a Biblical literalist.

In other words, two scholars may employ the same basic methods or techniques of interpretation and yet reach different conclusions because of differing presuppositions. The problem may not lie in the method at all. It is therefore unwise to criticize or condemn a Bible scholar solely because he uses some of the methods of historical critics or form critics. The unsatisfactory conclusions of contemporary form criticism may be caused by false presuppositions, while the methods themselves may be perfectly proper.

A second factor to keep in mind is that, as a general rule, the Bible student will find only applications which speak to his immediate situation and to his pressing needs. Only when he is personally and emotionally involved does genuine understanding and learning take place. His emotional involvement may consist of little more than a desire to understand God's will more fully. This desire is a basis for Bible study. Frequently, however, personal needs are apt to misdirect interpretation and application. The father with financial worries will instinctively find applications and perhaps even interpretations that help him meet his problem. The teen-age boy who is trying to reach a vocational decision will very likely find a different application than that which his worried father had found.

Applications which speak to personal needs are most likely to be remembered. And meaningful applications will also increase interest in Bible study. But this personal involvement can easily lead to abuses.

A glaring example of overly subjective use of the Bible is represented in the common practice of opening the Bible at random, pointing to a verse in the same way, and then interpreting and applying this as the basis for all the decisions of that day. Similar to this is the practice of what might be called "one-eyed interpretation." The reader takes a quick squint at a Bible verse, finds a word or phrase which appears to be meaningful to him, and then closes the Bible and goes his way, convinced that God has given him a special message.

The Truth, the Whole Truth, and Nothing But . . .

If all these personal, emotional, and philosophical elements affect Biblical interpretation, how can one be sure that he has understood the meaning, the whole meaning, and nothing but the meaning? This is the crucial question to which this book has addressed itself.

We must remember that these personal emotional elements, so long as they are normal and reasonable, are a part of the practice of Biblical interpretation. Let us note, too, that the principles and techniques described in Chapters 3 to 6 are designed to reduce the likelihood of subjective misinterpretation to a minimum.

We also need to keep in mind the great importance of determining as accurately as possible what the passage meant to the original hearers (the "then and there" meaning). This helps one to guard against the common error of reading into a text a meaning gained from other sources. Finally, we must immerse ourselves deeply in the contents of the Bible and have a clear grasp of its central message and consult with our Christian friends and with Christian Bible scholars and their commentaries.

Biblical Interpretation and Classroom Teaching

This course was written with a twofold objective in mind. The first was to help the reader develop his personal skills in Bible interpretation. The second objective was to enable the reader to understand how professional

Bible interpreters work and how they reach their conclusions. The achievement of these objectives to even a limited degree will provide church school teachers with invaluable know-how in the all-important task of Bible study. With some personal know-how, teachers will be freed from slavish dependence on a teachers manual or commentary. They may even find themselves disagreeing with others at times. Along with deeper personal convictions will come more freedom and power of the Spirit in ways of witnessing and teaching.

The development of personal skills of Bible interpretation will add measureably to the teacher's self-confidence. This seems to be one of the great needs of lay teachers. There is a great difference between saying, "This is what God says, because I read it in the teachers manual," and, "This is the truth of God's Word, because I know from my personal Bible study that this is the meaning." The pupils will sense the difference immediately.

The confidence that is gained by personal study will add the dimension of creativity, and this often makes the difference between a humdrum teacher and a good one. There will be new paths to explore and new ways of walking along old ones. The church school pupil's lament, "But we had all that before!" will be heard less frequently. Questions will be welcomed rather than feared, and often they will be thrown back to the questioner along with suggestions as to how he may find his own answer.

Teachers who are Bible students also teach with greater authority, the authority of the Word of God, rather than that of a lesson book or of a human being. Such a teacher can afford to be humble and respond with a cheerful "I don't know" to some questions. He will have learned that John Calvin was correct when he said that sometimes this is the only honest answer the Bible scholar can give to questions about Biblical meanings.

But isn't it quite idealistic to expect lay men and women to become Bible students? Won't it take hours of time to prepare lessons by carrying on one's own Bible study? The answer to both questions obviously is "Yes!" But several other things must be acknowledged before this basis of good teaching is rejected as impossible. Every church school teacher is called to teach and explain the Word of God and nothing but the Word. All teachers (ministers) of the church, lay as well as professional, have a high and sacred calling that demands careful and systematic preparation. Teachers can be certain that the investment of time in Biblical interpretation will pay handsome dividends for their task of teaching as well as for their private lives.

When a teacher immerses himself in Bible study and uses proper and productive hermeneutical principles, he himself grows in Christian grace and knowledge (2 Peter 3:18). As he sees in the Bible God's great plan for him, for His church, and for the world, he finds himself becoming more and more actively engaged as a living vessel of God's Word and Spirit.

This "being in God's Word" is contagious. The pupils catch it. They cannot, when confronted by teachers with personal convictions, just *passively* (intellectually) agree to truths (dead orthodoxy). They, too, find their minds and hearts and lives addressed by the Spirit of God and transformed by Him as they receive Him in faith.

It will be well to explain some of the principles of Biblical interpretation also to the older students in church schools so that they, too, can begin to experience the blessings of personal Bible study. Such teaching will help to create a generation of Christian leaders who will attempt great things for God in a world which is always desperately in need of the Gospel of Jesus Christ, the Word of life.

Summary

This chapter pointed out the vital connection which always exists between the teacher as a person, his personal faith and life, and his teaching. Bible study and interpretation is a basic key to a Spirit-guided and Spirit-empowered life in or out of the classroom. Sound Bible study requires the use of good principles and methods of interpretation and not merely the reading of the Book.

Three tasks of Biblical interpretation are investigation, reflection, and application. Careful use of hermeneutical principles helps a person discover the true meaning of a passage and keeps him from reading meanings into a text. Mastery of this kind of Bible study gives greater confidence to teachers and helps them confront their students with the authority of the Word and inspire them to believe and live the Christian faith more truly and fully.

TO HELP YOU REVIEW

1. Comment on some differences between Bible interpreters and Bible readers.

2. Summarize the purpose of each of the three basic tasks in Biblical interpretation.

3. How important is the guidance of the Holy Spirit in the study of the Holy Scriptures?

4. Explain what a presupposition is. What is the relationship between presuppositions, principles of interpretation, and the actual interpretation of a Bible passage?

5. Give examples of presuppositions which would affect the interpretation of Mark 5:1-20; Matt. 28:1ff; and Genesis 1.

6. What steps can you take to be sure that you are getting "the meaning, the whole meaning, and nothing but the meaning" of a given portion of Holy Scripture?

CONCORDIA LEADERSHIP TRAINING SERIES

Introductory Course

How You Too Can Teach: A Basic Preservice Training Course — Allan Hart Jahsmann